NOTHING GETS SOLD

—— UNTIL THE ——

STORY GETS TOLD

Corporate Storytelling
for Career Success *and* Value–Driven Marketing

STEVE MULTER

Message Master Media
700 W. Irving Park Rd., Ste A3
Chicago, IL 60613-3133

ISBN: 979-8-9857706-0-5 (paperback)
ISBN: 979-8-9857706-2-9 (ebook)
ISBN: 979-8-9857706-1-2 (hardcover)
ISBN: 979-8-9857706-3-6 (audiobook)

Ordering Information:
Special discounts are available on quantity purchases by corporations, associations, and others. For details, contact info@corporatestorytelling.com or +1 (312) 371-9640

This book is dedicated to my valued clients, colleagues, friends, and mentors in the events and global marketing industries. You have welcomed me in, shared your platforms, invited my partnership, fed and housed my family, sent me around the world and back again, and kept me in your warm company through every mile, meal, meeting, and message. I'm grateful for your wise council, the countless lessons you've shared over the last 25 years, and the inspiration you'll offer me over the next 25. I'm humbled to have served your needs as you have served mine.

Let's keep up the momentum, shall we?

CONTENTS

The trick is not just to get them to listen but to get them to act on what they have just listened to.

INTRODUCTION

WHEN IT COMES TO MARKETING COMMUNICATION, NO ONE LIKES to be sold to, but everyone loves a great story. Learn to tell a better corporate story, and you instantly create more value, passion, and connection for an audience, which pays off in big ways for you and your company. No matter your topic or audience size, or whether that audience is filled with strangers or colleagues, successful public presentation is the happy result of one simple and undeniable truth: nothing gets sold until the story gets told.

Corporate storytelling is an art and a skill that you can easily attain and leverage in every talk you deliver. Whether you are a seasoned, confident public speaker or one of the 73% who suffer from some degree of fear of public speaking (the most widespread and dominant phobia), adding corporate storytelling to your core content will transform your onstage presence. This book can help to turn your lecture into a conversation and your sales pitch into a memorable, actionable message.

Speakers who take the time and effort to look beyond what they are on stage to sell will measurably increase their value to—and connection with—an audience. It begins with understanding your viewer enough to recognize where their passions lie and how those passions align with your own—because until an audience recognizes why they should pay attention to you, they probably won't.

We attend a talk to hear what we want and need to hear, which is not always what a speaker chooses to tell us. To earn a viewer's investment in our marketing message, we need to place that message inside a recognizable and compelling story, one that is meaningful and inspirational to those viewers first and to ourselves second. Your talk has to be important to your audience in order to serve you and your reason for giving it. Tell them a good story, one that brings your data, metrics, and statistics to life, and your audience will get what they came to hear—which means they'll walk away from your talk inspired and motivated to take action on it.

Fortunately, turning your content into a strong corporate story is easier than you might think. When you tell us who you are and what you do, you should also tell us about your passion for the work you do and why you're so excited to share that passion for our benefit. When you explain your product, solution, or service, also help us to understand the amazing ways it can dramatically improve our status quo. When you demonstrate your technology, include your personal experience in a way that makes that technology so exciting; then we'll begin to get inspired about adopting it into our own daily lives. Pay as much attention to your corporate story as you do to your reason for telling it, then watch your audience gift you with their investment and enthusiastic response.

Type "corporate storytelling" into a search engine, and you'll find dozens, if not hundreds, of descriptions and interpretations of this common term that's taken root in modern-day presentation methodologies. Some take an overly academic view of the technique; for example:

> "Corporate storytelling designates private and public companies' and organizations' strategic utilization of stories and storytelling (in the broad sense of man's ability to tell and understand narratives) to create coherence and progression concerning the companies' or organizations' brand, identity and development."[1]

Okay. Technically, this is accurate, but it's drowning in corporate speak. The most concise encapsulation of corporate storytelling I've read comes

---

1   Norlyk, Birgitte, Marianne Wolff Lundholt, and Per Krogh Hansen. "Corporate Storytelling." *The Living Handbook of Narratology.* Interdisciplinary Center for Narratology, University of Hamburg. Revised September 2013. https://www.lhn.uni-hamburg.de/node/97.html.

from the principals at Anecdote International in *Corporate Storytelling—The Essential Guide*:

> "Corporate storytelling, also called business storytelling, is the purposeful and systematic application of story techniques in an organisation to deliver business outcomes."[2]

Again, technically accurate, but this is still too clinical for my taste. Simply put, corporate storytelling means combining the details of your topic with personal experiences that your audience can relate to, find value in, and become passionate about.

The first example of modern corporate storytelling is often credited to Deere & Company, a historic manufacturer of agricultural and forest machinery, heavy equipment, and diesel engines in the United States. In 1895, a decade after its founder's passing, Deere & Co. self-published a magazine called *The Furrow* that leveraged a then-revolutionary sales tactic, later identified as "content marketing."[3] Diverting from centuries of traditional product-centric rhetoric, Deere spoke directly to the farmers who used their products through intimate editorial communication. Instead of pitching tractors and plows, *The Furrow* told familiar stories of life on the land, painting a bucolic and recognizable picture of mutual value and shared personal meaning for new and established customers. It was an instant hit. By making sales subservient to the fostering of human connection and long-term business relationships, *The Furrow* launched a movement that continues to evolve even now.

---

2   Callahan, Shawn, Mark Schenk, Mike Adams, and Paul Ichilcik. "Corporate Storytelling—The Essential Guide." Anecdote. Accessed June 17, 2022. https://www.anecdote.com/corporate-storytelling.

3   Lo, Alan. "From 1895 and Beyond: John Deere's 'The Furrow' and Why Content Marketing Is Still Relevant Today." Stratwell Strategic Solutions. Accessed June 17, 2022. https://www.stratwell.ca/john-deere-the-furrow-content-marketing/.

A century later, I happened to find myself in a career that owes Deere & Co. a debt of gratitude. For the last 25 years, I've strategized, written, and delivered hundreds of corporate stories on behalf of some of the world's most powerful brands. Onstage, online, and on camera, I've given over 20,000 talks to more than two million clients and analysts. Along the way, I've collected a priceless treasure trove of best practices, gleaned in those conference halls, streaming broadcasts, and trade show exhibits. I'm eager to share the expert advice and first-person lessons I've learned from the most powerful keynotes and the most disappointing data dumps.

I'm also excited to share the great insights and experiences of sixteen fellow professional storytellers, friends, and colleagues. Between each chapter you'll hear their unique perspectives on how the right story can add value, passion, and connection to our lives. Every voice stands alone, but together they speak volumes on the power of great storytelling.

You may recognize yourself in these stories and throughout these pages, and you will certainly recognize the public speaking habits of others, both good and bad. On our journey, you'll discover proven tips, tricks, and insights that point to the payoffs of great corporate storytelling, and you'll learn numerous ways that you can quickly and easily apply them in every talk you give from now on. Once our eyes are opened to what good corporate storytelling can and should achieve, the proof is irrefutable. Average brands pitch; smart brands communicate. Time to rise above the average.

Every speaker is unique, which means that corporate storytelling is anything but one-size-fits-all. You have to reveal and craft the right story for yourself and your own organic presentation style. I tell every speaker I coach to take my suggestions on their merits, apply what makes sense, and discard the rest. I offer the same advice to you as a reader. Some ideas will feel right, while others will not. Some concepts will inspire you, while others may fall flat. But if you add even one new weapon to your public speaking arsenal, you will instantly notice the difference—and so will your audience. Then add another, and then another. You'll be delighted how quickly you become a better, more confident, and more successful corporate storyteller.

The first lesson in this book—the one that guides all other lessons that follow—is that no matter our job title, education level, income, or socioeconomic status, audiences all have one thing in common: they buy people first and products second. Before your listener will buy what you hope to sell, they first have to buy into you and your proposed value, your personal passion, and your undeniable connection to their way of thinking. You're going to hear these three words—value, passion, and connection—repeated and dissected again and again (and then again) throughout this book. And you're going to understand why.

Prove value for your audience with every word in your talk and every slide on your screen. Demonstrate genuine passion for your topic and why you believe others should be passionate about it too. Connect with your attendees as trusted friends and colleagues rather than as customers and contracts. These are the ways you turn a product pitch into a meaningful corporate story. And the better you become at corporate storytelling, the more your audience will buy you and your message. Because in the end, nothing gets sold until the story gets told.

CHAPTER ONE

THE POWER OF CORPORATE STORYTELLING

THINK OF THE LAST PRESENTATION YOU ATTENDED: THE UNCOMfortable chair, the generic conference room, the barrage of one dull data onslaught after another while you watched the clock and checked your phone. Think of the poor speaker on that stage, droning through yet another set of performance metrics and text-laden slides, aggressively explaining why their product is "the best," practically begging you to buy it. How much of their talk do you recall? How much passion did you hear in their story? Did you recognize a clear connection or compelling shared experience with that speaker? And did you receive enough personal or professional value to eagerly anticipate taking instant action the moment that speaker said goodbye?

We expect speakers to be heavy on numbers, details, key performance indicators, and corporate self-aggrandizement. Not because we prefer that style of presentation, but because, unfortunately, that typical content remains the grudgingly accepted norm. We all crave better corporate storytelling, but repeated letdowns naturally lead to lowered expectations. We want to hear better talks, but we seldom do. We want to deliver better talks ourselves but don't know how. For you, that changes right now.

The underlying differentiator between poor and compelling storytelling is whether a presentation is focused on companies and products or on people and personal values. In other words, is the speaker trying to make a sale or create a relationship? When a speaker simply pitches a product, touts their brand, and begs us to buy, they tell the wrong corporate story. But when that speaker proves deep value to their audience through personal passion and a shared human connection with those attendees, they tell the right corporate story.

In his best-selling book *Start with Why*, author and motivational speaker Simon Sinek explains, "People don't buy what you do; they buy why you do it. And what you do simply proves what you believe."[4] The best speakers recognize that, no matter how impressive their product, how celebrated their brand, or how compelling their proof point, their audience won't care about any of it until they understand exactly *why* that product, brand, and proof point will directly improve their lives in some meaningful way. As Sinek suggests, they won't care *what* you are on stage to sell or *how* that product or solution works until they know exactly *why* any of it matters to them.

You've seen a wealth of why-based corporate storytelling from superstar brands like McDonald's, Nike, Apple, Coca-Cola, BMW, Amazon, Progressive, Sony, and many more. Before these brands sell us their products, they sell us their story—a vision of a better tomorrow, one we dream of, hunger for, and aspire to. Connection with an audience (you and me) occurs when their brand vision directly and indisputably aligns with our personal wants and needs. When company and customer align, the message sticks and the stock soars.

Picture your favorite corporate brands, the ones you always seek out, select, and proselytize for, then ask yourself, "Why these particular companies or products instead of others?" You may believe that your preference is based solely on quality and performance. But it's more likely that your preference is linked to the stories those companies tell and the way their stories directly reflect your own. Preferring one mayonnaise to another is usually about taste; preferring one vehicle, airline, or software over another is usually about story.

---

4   Sinek, Simon. *Start with Why: How Great Leaders Inspire Everyone to Take Action.* New York: Portfolio/Penguin, 2009.

Strong storytelling brands can be outright poetic in their marketing. They paint glorious pictures of a smarter method, of unbridled success, or of a desirable achievement. These brands sell a vision of power, peace, pleasure, comfort, exclusivity, or wealth that hits our hearts and guts before it hits our heads. Once we imagine ourselves happily frolicking as the star in their beautiful pictures, their products become our doorway to achieving that reality for ourselves. It's a triple play combining value, passion, and connection into superior corporate storytelling.

Consider Apple, the world's most valuable brand.[5] Whether you love or hate the company's policies or products, no one can deny the effectiveness of their message or their perpetual societal and technical influence. Apple storytelling is not about practicality or awards or even product superiority; it's about emotion. The brand started with an invitation (and personal challenge) to "Think Different," not about the inner workings of a processor but about our combined global potential for limitless communication, connectivity, and access. Who among us doesn't want to be a part of that greater vision?

From the start, Apple offered an inspiring and humble college-dropout origin story, one that we can all find impressive and motivational. Steve Jobs and Steve Wozniak built a formidable community of rabid fans around their innovations in the early days, long before the general public knew who or what was about to dramatically and artistically alter the home computing landscape. To this day, Apple's creative advancements remain shrouded in secrecy, which only helps to keep that fanatical base growing, gossiping, and hungry for more.

Rather than market phones and laptops, Apple markets exclusivity and attitude, brilliantly built on perceived value. Their products may not be better than the competition's products, but their audience's perception of Apple's desirability, aesthetic superiority, and associated luxury leaves other players in the dust. Apple products are a status symbol, and customers care

---

5   Guerrieria, Martin. "What are the most valuable global brands in 2022?" Kantar BrandZ. June 15, 2022. https://www.kantar.com/north-america/inspiration/brands/what-are-the-most-valuable-global-brands-in-2022.

deeply about the status they display to the world. Apple makes its users feel good about their technology and about themselves, and when we feel good, we develop loyalty to the brand that delivers those positive feelings.

Even Apple's outbound marketing campaigns put the customer above the product. Every "Shot on iPhone" billboard focuses not on the details and data points of the built-in camera, but on the customers who took the image. Apple tells us *why* the camera matters to us, not *what* the specs are or *how* the camera functions. There are so many corporate storytelling lessons here. Your brand may not be as large or as rich as Apple, but your corporate storytelling can be every bit as good.

We see these lessons exemplified in numerous storyteller brands that focus on our collective goals and what makes us tick. They speak to our values, how we see ourselves, or how we *want* to see ourselves. Keep these concepts in mind as you begin to map out and construct your next public talk. Are you planning to paint a beautiful picture of success starring your audience, or are you planning to simply regurgitate data in a Legal-approved sales pitch?

Any time you speak on behalf of your organization, you'll be required to include key performance indicators (KPIs) and product details in your talk. This makes sense; your product or brand is the reason you've been asked to speak. But great corporate storytelling demands much more than an explanation of what you want to sell. Winning brands like Apple and Deere tell passion stories along with product stories. They balance data and detail with a compelling vision of a more perfect and satisfying future, one that conveniently features their product or service. Discovering passion for your corporate product or service may seem daunting, but we'll address that in later chapters.

To create your own winning talk is to create an opportunity that shows your listeners how much you care about them and their success, even above your own, and how closely your brand vision aligns with theirs. Every benefit you describe is a new picture of how your listeners can achieve that benefit for themselves. Every statistic is a handwritten invitation to new value and anticipation of reaching it. Every customer success story is a compelling vision of that brighter, easier, cooler future your guests have been secretly hoping for. Once they understand why your talk is about to change their lives for the better, you get to share what your product is all about and how it's built.

To reach this goal of stronger corporate storytelling, speakers and their organizations have to engage in unflinching self-assessment and more realistic understanding of how their marketing messages are perceived. This takes work and almost always challenges the status quo in uncomfortable ways. To tell the right story, a speaker has to know who they are speaking to and exactly what those people expect to hear. If the company is blurry on this key target, the speaker representing them will be equally out of focus.

This is not to suggest that a brand can't be successful without a good corporate story. Some do thrive by offering the right product at the right time, one that sells through distinction, singularity, or sheer design excitement. Remember the flurry for face masks in the first year of the COVID-19 pandemic?

In the internet age, mass distribution channels have created an endless marketplace for short-term get-rich-quick revenue generation that doesn't require corporate storytelling. Sixty seconds of flipping through any Facebook feed will net a dozen products that can be bought with a simple click and PayPal interaction. Most are offered at deep discount, designed for a narrow window of sales success. These aggregators don't need a story because they are not actually brands, just aisle cap offers amassed by tech-savvy cooperatives. The company makes their money in a flash, then flips to their next clearance item.

That's not you. When you give a talk, you represent a reputation, a positive customer experience, a plan for growth, and long-term success. The impact of great corporate storytelling on these goals can't be ignored. Yet it so often is. Some brands are so obsessed with their fragile bottom lines that they remain unwilling or unable to invest in strong corporate storytelling. Many companies labor under a toxic, ego-driven misconception that their product superiority is the only story worth telling. Others are convinced that enough hardcore marketing is all that is needed to drive acceptable profits. Eventually, any brand destined to last realizes that no one cares what they make or how they make it until they also recognize the story their brand tells the marketplace.

I've partnered with hundreds of organizations who've spent years or even decades minimizing their own *why* in favor of boring product pitches and underperforming hard-sell tactics. Finally, a new sales manager joins the organization and begins challenging the entrenched marketing rhetoric. Then they hire me to help transition from selling to communicating, and together, we begin building a better corporate story.

In my experience, the primary obstacle preventing brands from telling the right corporate story is a lack of trust. Executive leadership doesn't understand how their brand is perceived by the market and therefore doesn't trust that they need to change the message. Some don't trust their marketing team to tell a company story strong enough to sell the portfolio. Others don't trust that their brand's story is worth telling to begin with and that the product is the only worthwhile story. Perhaps they don't trust any metric beyond revenues to accurately measure the connection between brand and buyer, or they don't trust their audience to make the leap from corporate story to signed contract. By not trusting themselves or their customers, these brands have lost the narrative. These are the companies I am most excited to work with—and the ones that most need my help.

Every time I begin a new client partnership, we kick off with a probing and revealing question: Does your brand market to people or to corporations? Most have never thought about that distinction. Answers tend to range from "Huh?" to "What's the difference?" to "Both, I guess." It's a Pandora's box of self-assessment that leads to a vital brand-storytelling conversation. Once opened, that box is not easily closed.

As speakers, we get so wrapped up in satisfying industry analysts, quotas, and quarterly growth for shareholders that we never step back to consider the *people* we are actually speaking to. We don't contemplate the myriad ways in which we and our brand might benefit from constructing a larger and longer-lasting relationship with those we hope to reach. It's hard to think beyond the sale, all the way to the individual, because that requires personal investment in our talk instead of simple, safe reliance on preexisting marketing documentation. But that personal investment pays off by establishing commonality with our audience, and commonality is where meaningful professional and personal opportunities take root.

Commonality with an audience can open doors to new opportunities and ongoing professional relationships. In order to know and understand your viewers, you first have to know and understand why you're giving your talk and why you're asking them to attend. If you don't know why you're speaking or don't really believe in the value of what you have to say, your audience will feel that and check out. If you've forgotten what motivates you professionally or drives you personally, it's very hard to demonstrate passion for your topic, which then makes it far harder to elicit a passionate response from your audience.

Start by remembering why you chose to do what you do. Think of why you have earned the right to deliver this talk for the benefit of others. Feel the pride of your team, what you've accomplished together, and how you represent them as you speak. Picture the hopes and dreams of your viewers and the ways your values and theirs align and intersect. Imagine how their success will lead to your success. Build your talk with a combination of content and commonality, and you'll create a corporate story you can be proud to deliver. The content is the easy part; the commonality is what makes your message stick—and stick around.

These are the types of questions I ask my clients to ask themselves: Why was your brand created and what problem was it built to address? Is the original excitement and commitment to excellence that launched your company still clear and compelling? Where do your brand's current passions lie? How will those passions connect to and support any speaker you ask to deliver a talk on your behalf? Many companies can't remember back to their brand's founding or have forgotten the passion that first propelled them toward solving a specific market challenge. They still want to speak to an audience, but they have lost sight of their own narrative. I remind them that nothing gets sold until the story gets told, and then we get to work.

— BERNARD DERROITTE

Art Dealer | Art Historian | Climber

People don't buy the art; they buy the story.

A French auctioneer was known to bring down the hammer on something special with a signature phrase that never failed to delight his buying public. He'd yell, "Sold! The story, I mean. And I'll even throw in the work of art that goes with it!"

Despite appearances and perceived opinion, most works of art are not sold on the merits of their looks alone. A potential buyer is usually pulled in by something beyond visual cues, perhaps a subtextual beauty, a provocation, or a less obvious depth of messaging. In my experience, what sells a piece is more its nonvisible features than its visible ones. What sells a work of art is the story that goes with it.

Sometimes that story comes wholly from me, the dealer. Sometimes that story comes from the buyer. Sometimes both join forces to sow fertile collecting ground: my tale plus a personal legend in the mind of the buyer. Combining two great stories can even juxtapose two separate objects, where one ends up selling the other. In the end, valued art is valued art, but the story costs extra. That extra is how I make a living.

The story that sells a work may appear with the art itself, or it may require many hours of research and writing. Either way, when I spin a strong narrative for a work of art, it sells. It truly is as simple as that.

CHAPTER TWO

THREE PILLARS: VALUE, PASSION, CONNECTION

PRICEWATERHOUSECOOPERS INDIRECTLY OFFERS ONE OF THE clearest and most compelling arguments for what connects corporate storytelling to customer experience:

> Good customer experience leaves people feeling heard and appreciated. It minimizes friction, maximizes efficiency and maintains a human element.[6]

As a speaker coach, I've always been fascinated by how an audience actually "experiences" data, information, and marketing in a public presentation. What I've learned is that all viewers hear and evaluate incoming stimuli through three distinct filters and in a corresponding order of value: human first, consumer second, employee third. An audience will process, prioritize, and internalize content in this order. A speaker who recognizes and adapts to this innate hierarchy in the way information is consumed will reach an audience more successfully and in the right process of importance. As the flow of content becomes more satisfying for the audience, the

---

6   "Experience Is Everything. Get It Right." PwC. Accessed June 25, 2022. https://www.pwc.com/us/en/services/consulting/library/consumer-intelligence-series/future-of-customer-experience.html.

payoff for that speaker measurably increases.

This hierarchy remains universal despite our socioeconomic status, education level, or professional credentials. My longest client relationship has been with multinational technical giant Cisco Systems. Cisco's chairman and CEO, Chuck Robbins, is a remarkable and highly effective leader of roughly 80,000 global employees, overseeing a Fortune brand worth over $200 billion. At the time of writing, Mr. Robbins has a personal estimated net worth of $110 million, and he processes any marketing or sales messaging in exactly the same three-step order that you and I do.

Popular thought would suggest that the best way to market to Chuck Robbins, with his elevated level of power and responsibility, would be in purely corporate terms, through data points and dollar signs. Ultimately, these metrics are indeed what he uses to make his executive decisions. But initially, every decision he makes begins at home and not in Cisco's San Jose corporate headquarters on Tasman Drive. Before Chuck Robbins can assess any positive or negative choice for his corporation, he first assesses the direct impact on Chuck Robbins—and on his wife, his four children, the people he trusts, and the personal values that shape his life.

Want to sell something to Chuck Robbins the chairman and CEO? Start by selling it to Chuck Robbins the human being.

Value

We are perpetually inundated by tens of thousands of stimuli each day, a battlefield of attention-seeking messages all hoping to worm their way in and find a happy home in our hearts and wallets. Simply navigating our day-to-day existence, we arrive at any new marketing salvo pre-overwhelmed, already saturated by generic, indistinguishable products and endless bland sales ploys. Even the smartest among us simply don't have the time or bandwidth to fully consider every amazing offer and thrilling benefit flowing from such a relentless deluge of "Hey, look at me!"

As each new message arrives to compete for limited mindshare, we continually sort and distribute that data in knee-jerk determinations of "worth it" and "not worth it." The difference between those stimuli that cut through the noise and make an impact and those that go unheard or ignored is a psychological, emotional, and monetary game of *high-value* versus *low-value*. It's a subconscious assessment known in tech circles as "binning."

Picture how this moment-to-moment processing takes place within the folds of your cerebral cortex. In your processing brain are two hippocampi, one Cheeto-shaped area in each hemisphere where spatial memory and behavior memory are determined and where you decide what should be a short-term versus a long-term recollection. Inside those Cheetos, imagine four bins labeled "no-value," "low-value," "medium-value," and "high-value." As each new bit of stimuli arrives, it enters and moves across your cerebral cortex and into the hippocampus, where it is instantaneously assigned a label and gets summarily sorted into the corresponding bin.

Anything labeled "no-value" is never even seen, heard, or processed; it slips in and slips right back out again without registering, mentally or emotionally. *No-value* stimuli is pointless, vacuous soup, sloshing in the background but never tasted or noticed. Your *no-value* bin is limitless and vast because everything in it adds up to nothing. Your mind automatically empties the contents, like an auto-delete of mail from your junk folder, so there's always room to receive and then evacuate the next round of useless stimuli making up the majority of what you hear and see each day.

Items that reach your *low-value* bin are almost as easily ignored or forgotten. When they arrive, they may take an extra moment to process, but ultimately, they cause little more than a blip of mild interest before getting rapidly tossed into their own unworthy container. *Low-value* stimuli take up slightly more room, creating a sort of mental landfill. This forms a good foundation for comparison to better data, making it easier to distinguish and prioritize in comparison to the less useful flotsam.

Input that your hippocampal sorting mechanism perceives as *medium-value* sparks an interest and is deemed worthy of short-term storage for further evaluation. This data is still not a top priority, but you think, "Hmmm, there's something interesting here, perhaps some potential benefit worth exploration." These are the stimuli you set aside for now and hope to reconsider down the road after addressing items in your *high-value* bin. As you might have guessed, we rarely return to our *medium-value* bin content. Over time, that initial spark fades, and eventually most of those stimuli are relabeled "low-value" and discarded. Our thinking goes, "If I haven't done it by now, it must never have been that important to begin with."

Almost every message we encounter is deposited into our *no-value*, *low-value*, and *medium-value* bins. This is quite sad, really; after all the extensive marketing efforts, costly advertising investments, and studied strategic deployments, most brand messages go straight to our lesser bins. More often than not, the failure to connect can be directly attributed to bad storytelling, or to a complete lack of storytelling altogether. As you prepare for your next talk, your goal is to not end up in your audience's *low-value* or *no-value* bins.

The Holy Grail of all marketing messages and messengers is of course to reach the *high-value* bins in our listeners' minds. Precious few talks earn a coveted "high-value" label, and every storytelling brand on the planet is jockeying for that elusive spot. *High-value* input can speak to us personally, professionally, or both. And, just like Chuck Robbins, our audience will always process *high-value* on a personal level first and a professional level second. Even when the value of a talk feels more applicable to our career aspirations, we begin by assessing that value through our subconscious moral and ethical funnels.

Items in our *high-value* bins are those we embrace as top contenders for solving current problems, addressing immediate needs, clearing persistent obstacles, creating instant joy, or achieving imminent success. Any one of these goals is worth prioritizing, but if your message might help us achieve two or more of these payoffs, you'll rise to the top of our most valued bin. The sooner you redirect your talk from sales and data to commonality and passion, the sooner your content will be rewarded with *high-value* status.

Passion

Successful talks demonstrate genuine passion for solving your audience's most pressing problems. When your talk connects with your viewer through a mutually shared passion, you demonstrate the high value you place on them and on their personal and professional success. When your listeners recognize passion in you and your purpose for addressing them, they reward it with passion of their own.

Passionate messaging is just another way of saying "personal investment." Personal investment in your talk leads to a similar investment from your viewer, thanks to increased trust and shared values. It's not always easy to discover that passion and personal investment and then get it into your core content, but we'll cover that later.

Passion begins with strategic and dedicated removal of corporate speak whenever and wherever possible. At the time of writing, Wikipedia describes corporate speak as "the tone and style associated with large corporations, consultants, and governments that use unnatural and opaque language. It's often tedious and makes the meaning and intent of your talk unnecessarily difficult to understand, crushing passion and stifling natural conversation."[7]

Search your script for instances of corporate speak and replace them with your own words; natural and organic storytelling based on personal experiences and an emotional connection to your topic. For instance, look at the jargon in this passage:

> Lazarin is the first truly high-definition video communications company. We dramatically improve employee productivity and build relationships across distance by deploying high-quality, easy-to-use communication technologies that accelerate internal and external business operations.

---

7   https://en.wikipedia.org/wiki/Corporate_jargon.

This is pure corporate speak—empty and filled with buzzwords—that will net zero traction with an audience. Instead, replace it with:

> At Lazarin, we work with you to speed up your internal and external system operations. This lets your employees do their jobs better and really deliver for your customers. We like to call ourselves the first truly high-definition video communications company because our passion is helping partners like you build relationships with your clients, anywhere and everywhere. We know that technology can sometimes be more frustrating than helpful, so I'd like to show you how easy-to-use and affordable our technology is.

You see? Small edits can make a big difference. It's not so difficult to replace the corporate speak with personal investment that inspires and connects you with your viewer. Discard the mumbo jumbo in favor of a clear, compelling message built on genuine excitement for your topic and a vision of a mutually brighter future for both your audience and your industry. Your content will become more value-driven, and your listeners will remain engaged and enthused.

Passion will also drive action, the only true measure of success in any public talk. Smart brands (and the smart speakers representing those brands) add passion to their presentations in order to engage the audience, capturing their hearts and imaginations in ways that will motivate them to act immediately. The sooner you include passion in your corporate story, the sooner your listeners will positively and proactively respond.

Connection

With rare exception, we buy people before we buy products. Until we recognize ourselves in a speaker and their story, we won't hear or feel that story as our own. Until we internalize the value of a product in relation to our personal or professional lives, we won't invest our attention or our dollars. Until we feel the connection, we don't reward the message. As I said, we are all humans first and consumers second.

Connection between speaker and audience comes when a talk is delivered by one recognizable, accessible, trustworthy human sharing honestly and from the heart with a group of fellow humans. Connection never comes from a corporation speaking to nameless, faceless buyers. One communication method is about people; the other is about money. In order for a speaker to connect with a listener, they must demonstrate shared experiences, goals, and visions that prove commonality. Commonality builds trust in the speaker and their content, leading to mutual investment and success.

Getting more connection into your presentations requires a shift away from the typical information-heavy approach to scripts and slides. Generic product-centric marketing and hard-sell tactics are outdated, neglecting the fundamental truth that a good corporate story is not actually about you, your company, or your product; the best corporate story is about your audience.

Connecting with your listeners requires that you speak from their point of view instead of your own. Telling a better corporate story means redirecting your content away from you and your brand and outward to your listeners. Make them the star of your story, the focus of every data point and demonstration of product superiority. These redirects give you the highest possible chance of reaching your listeners' *high-value* bins.

Think of the speaker-audience connection as an equation: $S + A = P + I$.

Speaker + Audience = Passion + Inspiration.

The speaker (you) shares a compelling and motivating vision of a better, brighter tomorrow with the audience (fellow human beings), resulting in shared passion and inspiration. This equation should be applied to every public talk you give and assures mutual return on investment (ROI) for all parties.

You may view giving a talk as a joy or a grind; either way, it's always a gift. Any opportunity to speak to an audience deserves your personal investment, deep respect, and extraordinary care. Not only are you representing your corporation and its culture, but you are also asking others to set aside their hectic lives for a few minutes in order to prioritize you and the message you have to share. Keep that agreement firmly in mind, and think about how you plan to honor it, starting with a determination to make a real connection.

This is a choice. You can either deliver a data dump in corporate speak or connect with your attendees through a human story filled with shared interests, fears, visions, and victories. The former is likely to land you in your audience's *low-value* or *no-value* bins; the latter is your path to the *high-value* bin, based on mutual value and shared success.

Value, passion, and connection work together to align your story with their story, your pain with their pain, and your success with their success. Rather than mindlessly rattling off bullet points about your product to a skeptical field of potential customers, you'll offer your listeners a trusted friend instead of corporate shill. Fill your corporate story with recognizable experiences, inspiring successes, and embarrassing failures that humanize both you and your topic. You'll see the positive response in their faces and feel the enthusiasm in their follow-up actions. This is the natural give-and-take that defines a healthy speaker-audience relationship.

BRIAN HILLIGOSS

Production Manager | Musician | Raconteur

As a young musician and performer growing up in North Carolina, I discovered songwriting as a way to tell stories. I would sit, cross-legged, over layers of LP jackets that cluttered my bedroom floor and wear out vinyl recordings of Grand Ole Opry greats like Hank Williams Sr., Porter Wagoner, and Roy Acuff. As they spun tales of lost love and country lore, I'd teach myself to play "I'm So Lonesome I Could Cry" and learn to yodel just like Hank. How could these storytellers be so profound using such simple words?

Eventually, I made the move to Nashville and, within a few months, stood on those hallowed boards of the Grand Ole Opry myself, about to take the stage as rich sound swirled through that cavernous theater and butterflies flitted in my stomach.

As I waited for "The King of Country Music," Mr. Roy Acuff, to introduce me—me?—to a full house of country music fans, a mature, aristocratic, Southern belle voice whispered into my ear. "Are you nervous?"

I turned to see the legendary storyteller and comedienne Minnie Pearl, with a wide grin on her face and a $1.98 price tag dangling from the brim of her hat. "Yes, ma'am, I am," I stammered back.

She took my hand, squeezed it softly, and leaned in close. "Just love 'em," she said, "and they'll love you back."

The right story lasts a lifetime.

CHAPTER THREE

THE SPEAKER–AUDIENCE RELATIONSHIP

EVERY SPEAKER WANTS THEIR TALK TO SUCCEED. THEY WANT THEIR audience to listen, learn, respond positively, and take action on the content of their talk. At the same time, every audience wants that speaker's talk to be a success. They hope for a clear and compelling reason to lean in, to give focus and enthusiasm for a presentation that offers valuable information and conveys passion. On paper, this relationship sounds straightforward; each party is aware of, and dedicated to, their specific role in the speaker-audience interaction. The arrangement should be efficient and mutually beneficial. But it so rarely is.

The last time you were asked to give a public presentation for your company, your congregation, or maybe in defense of a term paper, how did you respond to that request? Or was it less a request than a "voluntold" expectation? Were you excited for the opportunity to share your story or struck by a sickening drop in the pit of your stomach? Were you eager to start crafting your talk right away or desperate for a viable excuse to politely decline? Speaking in public, for personal or professional reasons, elicits a range of emotions spanning from egotistical glee to crippling anxiety. Statistically, most of us skew toward the anxiety end of the spectrum, which is why the supposedly simple speaker-audience relationship is anything but. Where you line up on the gleeful–anxious spectrum is likely a product of both personality and experience, both innate and cultivated.

"Innate" because roughly 73% of us suffer from some form of what social science refers to as glossophobia,[8] a Latin mash-up of "tongue" ("glossa") and "dread" ("phobia") that combine to form the leading globally shared human panic: fear of public speaking. Modern experts in the fields of psychology and psychiatry prefer the term "social phobia" to define a more general fear centered around social situations and interactions, with fear of public speaking as one element. But it's the element everyone knows and self-ascribes.

In his 1998 special, *I'm Telling You for the Last Time*, Jerry Seinfeld articulated fear of public speaking with remarkable clarity and wit: "I saw (a) study that said speaking in front of a crowd is considered the number one fear of the average person. Number two was death. This means, to the average person, if you have to be at a funeral, you would rather be in the casket than doing the eulogy."

"Cultivated" because many of us start our lives gleeful about performing in public, then begin the slow drip toward glossophobia. At the age of four, we can't wait to put on a puppet show or rock concert for our family and friends. A decade later, we'd rather walk across hot coals than be thrust into the spotlight. The perceived risks of failure become greater with time and self-awareness, eventually leading to glossophobia.

This subtle transition begins in primary and elementary school, where we first learn to worry that speaking out of turn or answering incorrectly might cause embarrassment. If we say the wrong thing, others might think we're stupid. The stakes increase through middle and high school when misspeaking can brand us as uncool or unpopular: a loser. The cute guy or girl won't pay attention to us, or the bully will use our failures to mock us. In movies, the awkward teen makes their presentation, and the class laughs, shaking their heads in derision. Fears build through university and early career positions when a poor public talk could threaten our odds at that scholarship, dream internship, raise, or desired leg up we so

---

8   Montopoli, John. "Public Speaking Anxiety and Fear of Brain Freezes." National Social Anxiety Center. Accessed June 25, 2022. https://www.nationalsocialanxiety-center.com/2017/02/20/public-speaking-and-fear-of-brain-freezes/.

desperately crave. By the time we are fully immersed in the workforce, we've acquiesced to a sad but undeniable reality that speaking in public usually runs a higher risk than keeping our mouths shut and our heads down, flying safely under the radar.

Yet, in this same workforce, we face a parallel reality that constantly tests our fear of public speaking. Like it or not, most of us have to deliver presentations. It's often a mandatory aspect of our jobs. Professionally, we are required to speak even if, personally, we loathe and hope to avoid it. No wonder the speaker-audience relationship is strained. But while we may not look forward to giving a talk, we also don't have to feel like throwing up each time we approach a microphone.

If 73% of us are glossophobic by nature, who are the exotic and confusing 27% who actually enjoy public speaking? And why? This minority spans their own spectrum, from relaxed acceptance to enthusiastic anticipation. Most do not quite love giving presentations, but neither do they fear the experience or shy away from it as so many of us do. A scant minority are truly excited and evangelistic about public speaking; I happen to be one of them.

My strange predilection toward the effusive, gregarious, and dramatic was apparent from the age of five. Getting me to speak in public was easy; getting me to shut up was the challenge. Some say it still is. My evolution to a career in public speaking at the age of 30 surprised no one, but it took another 10 years before I became what I'd call "good" at it. Talk by talk and event by event, my natural proclivities evolved into telling better stories on stage, and today my love of speaking is stronger than ever. I continue to discover deeper emotional and personal payoffs through sharing value with rooms full of strangers and colleagues. I am always grateful to guide others toward the incremental conquering of glossophobia, helping them tell better, more confident stories and create more personal or professional success.

Whether you are a persistent glossophobic or a recent award winner in your local Toastmasters chapter, every successful talk starts with understanding and accepting your audience, then delivering for them. If your talk fails to spark their interest and lacks clear value, they will forget your message the moment you finish speaking. But if your talk gives them what they want to hear and delivers the value they crave, they will reward you by acting on your content. That audience-speaker relationship is almost entirely up to you.

Glossophobia gets in the way of that speaker-audience balance by eroding confidence and therefore value. If the speaker is not confident in their ability to successfully communicate or in the level of value they can realistically bring to a talk, the audience will hear and feel something's missing and respond in kind. When an audience senses insecurity or hesitation from a speaker, it translates to a perceived skepticism about the value that speaker is likely to provide. The speaker then perceives the audience's concern, and the downward spiral begins.

Consider this alternate perspective: If you are afraid to speak in public, so are your viewers. In other words, while today you are the one on stage worried about failure, they will be the ones equally worried tomorrow when it's their turn to speak. Your glossophobia is theirs and vice versa, which already creates commonality. When I'm coaching insecure speakers, I tell them, "Remember, they're just happy it's you up there giving the talk and not them!"

The greatest enemy of glossophobia is value. Value creates confidence, for you and for your listeners. When you know that your talk is valuable to your audience, you strengthen the speaker-audience relationship regardless of your natural glossophobia. Tell a better story, and trust and confidence will reign, no matter what insecurities might linger behind the voice.

Let's support that assertion with a bit of science. A 2014 study from *Frontiers in Human Neuroscience* points to the underlying cause of glossophobia as being rooted in fear of negative evaluation, or FNE.[9] FNE can modulate electrocortical and behavioral responses when anticipating

---

9   Van der Molen, Melle J. W., Eefje S. Poppelaars, Caroline T. A. Van Hartingsveldt, Anita Harrewijn, Bregtje Gunther Moor, and P. Michiel Westenberg. "Fear of Negative Evaluation Modulates Electrocortical and Behavioral Responses When Anticipating Social Evaluative Feedback." *Frontiers in Human Neuroscience* 7 (January 2014). https://doi.org/10.3389/fnhum.2013.00936.

potential negative social evaluative feedback. In other words, our glosso-phobia stems from fear of judgment from, or negative evaluation by, others. Worrying what other people think of us leads us to stifle and suppress our personal stories, as detailed by the National Social Anxiety Center[10] and National Institute of Mental Health.[11]

Several years ago, on a flight from Chicago to San Francisco, I was seated next to a lovely gentleman in his mid-sixties named Eric. While the plane taxied, we began making small talk, and Eric asked where I was headed and why. I told him that I'd spent over 20 years as an executive speaking coach and corporate spokesman for Fortune and cutting-edge global brands and that I was winging west to present for one of those brands at a large industry event. Eric was fascinated.

He revealed that his lifelong goal had been to become a public speaker himself, specifically as a minister in his church, but that he had lacked the courage to realize his dream. In his late teens and early twenties, Eric had not believed his stories or personal perspectives had "enough" to offer or that they would be interesting or meaningful in ways that could engage a congregation. He convinced himself that he had nothing of value to say, and that he was too dull to say anything that anyone truly wanted to hear. Glossophobia suppressed Eric's confidence, creating an irrational and inaccurate fear of judgment from, or negative evaluation by, others. Sadly, I hear Eric's story all too often from people I work with and those I meet in planes, trains, and automobiles.

Eric attended university in Illinois and earned a master's in engineering and aeronautics. He spent over 40 years in a remarkable career, working on the International Space Station and F-22 Raptor, among other projects. He married young, raised a family, and lived all over the world. Then, one year into retirement, on a motorhome trip through Alaska with his wife, Eric was faced with a crisis of conscience. He was asked by his church to head

---

10   "Public Speaking Anxiety." National Social Anxiety Center. Accessed June 25, 2022. https://www.nationalsocialanxietycenter.com/social-anxiety/public-speaking-anxiety/.

11   LaDouceur, Pat. "What We Fear More Than Death." MentalHelp.net. Accessed June 25, 2022. https://www.mentalhelp.net/blogs/what-we-fear-more-than-death/.

up a community outreach program for financially-challenged and starving encampments in Asia, an effort that would involve constant public speaking. For Eric, this was his true come-to-Jesus moment.

After four decades suppressing his original dream, and despite continuing reluctance, Eric had finally gained enough perspective and experience to see it was time to set those fears aside and realize his lifelong goal. Glossophobia be damned. Today, Eric heads an extensive outreach ministry across small community congregations in remote villages that run from the Arctic Circle down through Russia, central Asia, and eastern China. He gives talks every day and knows he always has something valuable to say. Embracing that personal value gave Eric the confidence to connect with his audience. It also gave Eric's audience the confidence to fully invest in him and his message.

It took Eric over 40 years to realize what I want you to realize reading his story—and before four decades of your own life go by. When it comes to public speaking, most of us are so busy negatively judging and evaluating ourselves that we don't have the time or energy to negatively judge or evaluate others.

Speakers and audiences are allies, not adversaries. The next time you are asked to give a public talk, whether it's for two people, 200, or 2,000, trust that your audience *wants* you to succeed. How do you know that? Ask yourself, "When someone gets up to speak in front of me, do I instantly start judging them negatively, or am I giving them my support and optimism? Am I looking for them to fail, or am I encouraging them to succeed?" What you want for any other speaker is precisely what they want for you.

My earliest lessons on the speaker-audience relationship began in Phoenix, around my grandmother's table. Jeannette Multer was a fabulous and formidable lady—wickedly smart, curious, well-traveled, and dazzlingly well-read. Grandmother (never Grandma, Granny, or Nana) was a powerful mentor long before I knew what a mentor was or how lucky I was to have one in my life.

Growing up in San Diego, the child of divorced parents in the early

1970s, I spent each August with my grandparents, swimming, sipping iced tea, and sheltering from sandstorms and heat lightning through languid 115-degree Arizona days. Grandmother and Hum (my oldest cousin couldn't say "Grandpa Herman" as a toddler, so Herman became Hum to all he knew) lived at 70 East Ashland, right across from the Pepto Bismol–pink Church of Jesus Christ of Latter-day Saints, a fine location for any good Jewish family. The house had no air conditioning, so Grandmother would fill my bed with trays of ice cubes while tucking me in at night. The ice would melt and evaporate as I drifted off to sleep. This was my second home.

On holidays and special occasions, the entire family would travel from multiple cities to gather around Grandmother's table, eating, drinking, laughing, and talking at each other. Not *with* each other, *at* each other; Jews know how to talk. Everyone had a story to tell, but not every story found its audience. I was the youngest and less interested in adult conversation than in slipping bits of food under the table to Yogi, my grandparents' dog.

As the years and holidays passed, and I got a bit older, I started to recognize an intriguing dynamic around that table, the first inklings of a psychological experiment forming in my young mind. Grandmother was always seated by the kitchen doors, while Hum anchored the other end by the living room. As competing stories flew, there was a reliable pattern to who commanded attention and who suffered from lack of audience engagement. I had no perspective to assess the reasons for success and failure in these speaker-listener relationships, but the die was cast; for some reason, I was fascinated.

It didn't seem to matter if the *content* of one story was more interesting and another less so, or if one speaker was more naturally entertaining than another; the difference was in the passion of the storyteller. Some of my family members had a great deal of passion, while others had none. When the storyteller was passionate, speaking with energy and enthusiasm, my family was all in. When the speaker was just talking to hear themselves talk, my family checked out. It was a light bulb moment, though I wouldn't know why for many years.

When it came to passionate storytelling, nobody held court like Grandmother. Not only was she the matriarch and principal pillar of our family, she almost always had something genuinely valuable and meaningful to say. This meant Grandmother always enjoyed the most rapt listeners. Her speaker-audience connection was undeniable. Others in my family were less successful.

One Thanksgiving, my Aunt Stephanie, Grandmother's daughter and my father's only sibling, was telling a story to my dad across the table. The meal was over, and I was slipping scraps to an even older and lazier Yogi when, midsentence, my father got bored with his sister's narrative and callously abandoned her. One minute Aunt Stephanie had an audience; the next moment that audience turned its gaze to Grandmother's story at the other end of the room. My aunt was adrift, hanging in the ether, discarded and incomplete. The woman never missed a beat. For the next two minutes, she finished her story to the side of her brother's head. He was utterly unaware she was still speaking to him, but that didn't matter; Aunt Stephanie had her narrative, and she was intent on delivering it whether or not her listener cared. It was mesmerizing. Over time, I would come to learn that this is how most speakers deliver their talks, barreling ever onward through content that their audience no longer hears or cares about.

I loved my aunt, but holding an audience was not Stephanie's strong suit. Her mother was just the opposite, each story filled with commitment and a genuine belief that she had value to offer her audience. This unintended social experiment, juxtaposing two powerful women in my young life, was seminal.

The lesson they unintentionally imparted was that not every talk has to be delivered by an expert speaker in order to succeed. Grandmother was no professional storyteller, but her passion was the key to creating a valuable speaker-audience connection that won attention and investment. Aunt Stephanie was brilliant and beloved, but her stories lacked the passion of her mother's, which left her listeners less engaged and more disconnected from the narrative. We should all strive to be more like Grandmother.

I share this story because your family is probably a lot like mine. And because family stories are, technically, rarely the greatest ever told. But for most of us, our family's stories help to form who we will eventually become. Imagine if the people in your family had been too afraid to tell their stories around the Thanksgiving table out of fear of judgment or negative evaluation.

Every talk you give, on any subject, in any venue, for any audience, has the potential to make a positive impact on a fellow human being, as Grandmother's stories did on me. Like her, you just need to offer genuine value in service to your listener. Once you commit to delivering value for the benefit of others rather than for yourself or your company, you'll begin boldly pushing past your glossophobia. And you'll minimize any concern that others are negatively judging or evaluating your presentation.

Think of a memorable story you heard at some point in the past. Perhaps it was last week, last year, or when you were a child—whatever pops into your head. A story that made you smile or infuriated you or gave you inspiration or made you cry. Now think of the person who told you that story. Can you still hear their voice in your head, see their face, or feel the passion in their words? Was the storyteller who gave you that gift of emotion an expert speaker? Or was that storyteller just a normal person like you or me?

Your talk might make someone's job easier or their company more successful. You could help them overcome an obstacle. Or, as with Eric, you could inspire them to realize a lifelong dream. When your talk delivers recognizable, clear, undeniable value, there is no room for judgment from, or negative evaluation by, others. There is only you, your audience, your passion, and your desire to share your experience for the benefit of those around you.

You don't have to be an expert storyteller for your talk to achieve success. Odds are that your parents, grandparents, cousins, and aunts aren't expert storytellers, just average, wonderful people who speak from the heart and share their ideas. Their stories remain with you for a lifetime, a perfect example of the potent and natural speaker-audience alliance.

Embrace that relationship. Remember that value comes from you and your personal story, not from your solution or service. Focus on your audience and on what they most want and need to hear. Prove to your listeners that you are on stage or on camera for their glory and benefit more than for your own. Balance the product content and data dumps with human connection that demonstrates shared values and perspectives. Trust that they want you to succeed.

Once you learn to trust your audience, you inspire their trust in you. Rather than judge or negatively evaluate you and your talk, your audience will follow wherever you lead them. As you begin to add value, passion, and connection to your next talk, your faith in your ability to successfully communicate will grow. And, in turn, your glossophobia may start to recede. You'll be left with more opportunity to embrace a few of the other prevalent global fears that make our lives interesting: necrophobia (death), arachnophobia (spiders), agoraphobia (outdoors or crowds), trypanophobia (needles), acrophobia (heights), mysophobia (bacteria or germs), or ophidiophobia (snakes). Is your natural glossophobia also accompanied by one or a few of these? If so, you should be one hell of an interesting storyteller!

STEPHANIE ROGERS

Band Leader | Trainer | Singer/Songwriter

It's May 2021, and I'm coaching a team of bank employees. Coronavirus deaths are on the rise, jobs have been lost, morale is low, and no one wants to be stuck in yet another mandatory Zoom class. I cheerfully ask the group, "Who wants to do a warm-up exercise?" Several participants switch off their cameras. "Could everyone please unmute and turn your cameras on?" They don't. So, I change the conversation.

"Look, I'm just gonna share a true story, OK?" I tell them about the four-year-old boy who showed up at our house on Halloween in 2001 to ask if my husband and I would take him trick-or-treating. His smile was as big as the sun. We asked about his family and slowly learned that his mother had abandoned him, his father had been killed in gang violence, and he lived with his depressed grandmother, who made him sleep on the couch while she smoked and watched horror films. We brought the boy trick-or-treating with us that night, side by side with our son.

Last week, the doorbell rang again. That sweet boy was a brand-new college graduate, home to celebrate his 24th birthday with the family who'd finally adopted him. Together, we looked through old Halloween pictures and realized how a little love can create a big future.

My whole story took less than 99 seconds to tell. A moment later, one of the bankers unmuted to say that he wouldn't have survived if it weren't for the family who adopted him. Then another camera switched on, and a young woman professed her lifelong dream to foster a child. Eventually, every person returned, revealing their stories of mentoring, fostering, or adopting kids. This diverse team of executives had worked together for three years without knowing this remarkable thing they had in common.

How do we make connections and build bridges? We share our stories.

CHAPTER FOUR

UNDERSTANDING AND DELIVERING FOR YOUR LISTENER

GETTING MORE VALUE INTO YOUR TALK STARTS WITH A GENUINE desire to tell a better story. A better story comes from understanding who you are speaking to and why, then committing to communicating from their point of view instead of your own. Until then, the value equation is one sided, entirely in favor of the speaker. This is the fundamental problem with most talks you've attended. My advice to speakers is "Don't tell them what you want to tell them; tell them what they want to hear."

Speakers tend to talk about what *they* want to talk about, with little thought for who is on the receiving end. Any value in their story is likely inwardly focused, centering on what they deem valuable to themselves or to their own brand: "It matters to me, so it should matter to my audience." But what a brand finds most valuable about itself—its products, history, recognition, awards, and market share—is rarely of paramount value to the listener.

Marketing departments refer to this as the WIIFM factor: What's in it for me? "Me" in this acronym is meant to represent the listener's perspective on whether or not a story holds value and is, therefore, worthy of their continued attention. You may have heard a slight variation on this theme as

WIIFT: What's in it for them? Either way, the intent is the same. Applied correctly, WIIFM or WIIFT should compel any marketer or salesperson to prioritize audience interests and perspectives above those of the storyteller. Unfortunately, most presentations miss that mark. They misinterpret "me" to mean themselves, a justification that what matters most to the audience *should be* what the brand itself deems most important about its own product. In other words, "What's in it for me is more sales, commissions, and profit!"

If I believe my company's product is "the best," then I am likely to focus most of my talk on that product. I assume my audience will easily understand my pitch, quickly recognize and accept my product's superiority, and purchase it for their own benefit. Using this inward-looking perspective, the power of my solution is what I believe is "in it" for them.

By that same logic, if my audience is excited by my product and decides to buy it, that satisfies my own expectation of "what's in it for me." This strategy makes the egotistical assumption that both parties clearly see what's "in it" for one another, so the logical outcome should be larger sales and higher revenues. Are you feeling the passion in that equation? Nope, me neither.

The primary goal for most speakers is simply to get their audience to pay attention, then sign a contract. But this assumes the audience's primary goal in attending a speaker's talk is to find a contract to sign. That is a losing strategy, and the talk is destined for the viewer's *low-value* or *no-value* bins.

This approach also explains why so many of us prefer not to speak in public. If making a sale is the typical, expected, and accepted reason for giving a talk, then the only measure of success is whether the audience buys our product once we finish the presentation. But nobody likes to be sold. You don't like it as the speaker, and neither does the attendee hearing you speak. Selling from the stage is therefore an open door to glossophobia.

Wise use of WIIFM/WIIFT doesn't focus on the product or the pitch but on how to best serve and support each individual in the room. Your audience is the only party allowed to ask "What's in it for me?" And the only "in it" that matters is the one that helps your audience members achieve their unique visions for personal or professional success. Make my mantra into your mantra in every talk you deliver from now on:

*Don't tell them what I want to tell them;
tell them what they want to hear.*

Only most speakers don't know what their audience wants to hear. Worse, they often don't care. It's nothing personal, just the result of general reluctance to give a talk, a debilitating lack of bandwidth, or a misunderstanding of what truly matters to their viewers. Any or all of these factors can lead a presenter to underdeliver for the sake of expediency or perceived shortage of time in the calendar. These obstacles are understandable. They're also detrimental to good corporate storytelling and easily overcome.

Most of us who are asked to give presentations already have full-time jobs with high expectations, long hours, and expanding quotas. This leaves little extra time for public speaking or proper preparation. Glossophobic or not, being assigned to deliver a talk is usually a burden rather than a privilege. Here is how that burden tends to play out.

We commit to our jobs for the paycheck, not the passion. Without genuine passion for the position, it can be difficult to demonstrate passion in any scripted content. From that baseline, most speakers are not properly trained by their companies in how to tell the most value-oriented brand story. This is hardly surprising, since so many brands don't know or understand that brand story themselves. The company requests (or demands) that we prepare for a new talk—an added expectation with no added pay—and we enter the ring with one hand tied behind our backs. We know our topic, but we don't really have the time to do it justice. We also don't know how our superiors would like it to be delivered.

Even if we're excited to give the presentation, regular demands on our already full-time position don't diminish. With little or no spare mindshare outside business hours to fully embrace this new opportunity, options for speaker preparation are few and far between. Devoting time to the crafting and rehearsing of a talk requires either cutting corners at work or cutting into personal time with family and friends.

Meanwhile, content expectations from higher up the command chain are far too prescriptive. We're not truly free to talk about what we hope to talk about or about what the audience wants and needs to hear from us. Leadership commands that our talk contains piles of specific data, statistics, and Legal-approved documentation. Stifled by predetermined demands, there's no time left for personality, passion, connection, or audience value. Edge-to-edge product and technical details fill the entire time slot, and the attendees become the lowest priority. What's in it for them? Precious little. What's in it for the company? Reduced odds of success. What's in it for the speaker? More work, added stress, and minimal creativity.

If you've ever wondered why so many of the sessions you attend are disappointing, uninspiring, and a waste of everyone's time, now you understand the sad process that led to that bad result.

Speakers can be hamstrung from the start, despite expertise in their topic and an optimistic plan to share a strong presentation with their audience. I call this "communicating from the paycheck." A successful talk demands that you control and create your own story, built on your own approach to content and the personal experience only you can offer that brings that corporate story to life for your attendees. When someone else tries to assert authority over your talk, I urge you to resist; remind those authorities that you are the one giving the talk, which means you are the one ultimately responsible for its success.

And it's not just company employees who face these challenges. Often, the speaker is a C-suite executive supported by another employee further down the corporate ladder, someone assigned to gather content then create the script and slides for their boss to deliver. This content is usually laden with words that feel inorganic or uncomfortable in the speaker's mouth, adding stress for the presenter and fomenting disconnection from the audience.

This weak presentation cycle repeats and repeats in endless hotel ballrooms, numbing Zoom calls, and forgettable conferences. Despite the best intentions, most talks fall flat because the speaker is unwilling or unable to control their own content or incorporate passion into their communication, or flails under the weight of their own overwhelming time demands. You can break that cycle, starting with a plan to tell a better story and to build that story correctly from day one. Getting your story off on the right foot honors your calendar and other job requirements, minimizes the impact on your valuable time, and delivers maximum payoff for both you and your audience.

Ask Pregame Questions

An old adage warns that a stitch in time saves nine. Less poetically, if you put in the work up front, you save far more effort down the road. Most of us dive into scripting or slide design without a plan, based on preexisting data and statistics alone with no story or structure to give that data meaning. With too little time in our calendars to do more, we seek a fast path to completion. While expediency seems justified, the truth is that lack of preparation actually consumes far more of our time and effort, not less. Investment in solid pregame preparation, before putting pen to paper or fingers to keyboard, will save you many stitches later in the process.

Begin by asking yourself a few key questions about your topic, your purpose for giving the talk, your goals, and your audience's reason for attending:

- *What am I up on that stage to say about myself, my passion, and my brand?*
- *How can I most effectively serve my market?*
- *What is my audience looking forward to hearing from me?*
- *How will my content be a worthwhile exchange for their time and attention?*
- *What can I say that my audience can actually apply and benefit from right away?*
- *How can I help my audience achieve something powerful and useful?*
- *What can I offer to make my talk stay with them long after my limited time on stage?*

Any speaker who takes the time and care for this honest assessment—before writing or slide design—is showing respect for both the occasion and the audience's investment. Honoring your listeners' needs before your own is how you add those first elements of undeniable value into your corporate story.

And from a self-serving perspective, asking and answering these types of WIIFM/WIIFT questions early on sharpens your focus and increases your odds of delivering a successful talk. This initial assessment will help you to craft your script and slides with a clearer vision of your purpose and key targets. It also launches you toward a stronger, more confident story and gets you to that story in less time and with less struggle.

Right away, you are going to gain greater insight into the true heart of your brand and what makes it beat. You will grasp *why* you do *what* you do. You will clarify your most valuable and meaningful core differentiator in an overcrowded marketplace full of *low-value* propositions. Most important, you are more likely to understand how you can truly serve your market rather than just sell to it. Understanding your audience and delivering what they want is the fastest and surest path to the *high-value* bin.

These revelations also extend beyond the talk itself. The better you understand your own brand and the passion that drives it, the deeper the value you can create and deliver for your viewers. That expanded value embeds your message more deeply, which helps listeners carry more of it away with them once you've left the stage. As you reveal and respect why you do what you do, you will inspire others with a visible pride of purpose for your own company and its people. When your work means so much to you, it will mean so much more to your listener.

Challenge Yourself Throughout Content Production

Those pregame questions shouldn't just be asked once but over and over again as you construct your talk, from the very first word of your presentation through to the last. Constantly challenge your own content for value, focus, and clarity.

- ❑ *Is each piece of my talk demonstrating passion for my topic?*
- ❑ *Will my listeners be inspired through each section of this talk?*
- ❑ *Am I still focused squarely on what I hope to accomplish for my valued guests?*
- ❑ *Is the story being told from my audience's point of view or my own?*
- ❑ *Am I giving my attendees exactly what they've asked me for?*
- ❑ *How am I addressing their biggest challenges instead of my own?*
- ❑ *Is my content providing them with clear, simple ways to overcome their obstacles?*
- ❑ *Am I being clear and compelling or rambling and going too deep into the weeds?*
- ❑ *Is this story motivating enough to get my audiences to take action?*
- ❑ *Am I offering every tool they'll need to take that action quickly and easily?*

Questions like these (and the ones you create for yourself) will continually inform scripting decisions, serving as guardrails that ensure every idea, every data point, and every slide, image, and graphic you share on-screen are for your audience's glory and benefit. "Know as you go" is a recipe for success, saving you time and stress. Apply your questions line by line and page by page to ask if your script is striving to communicate or only to make a sale. If it's the latter, change your strategy before moving on to the next sentence or paragraph.

This self-interview exercise will also save you time and effort across your talk development process. Skip it, and you'll have far more work to do later on in edits and rewrites. When every part of your corporate story serves the primary goals that you have laid out for yourself, you eliminate any question of whether your listeners will be glad they invested their time and attention in you. Knowing each word of your talk contains value and respect for your audience reduces the risk of losing their attention, which then reduces your risk of experiencing glossophobia.

Practice on Existing Content

Here is a quick and painless exercise. Search your files and pull up the last talk you gave. If you have never given a public talk, look for a recent internal company presentation or university course syllabus. Begin with the opening statement and speak the first page of your content. Now challenge that scripting with revealing questions like these:

- *Does the talk open with value so the audience has a reason to give it their full attention?*
- *From the start, is the script telling the company story or the listener's story?*
- *How often does the speaker talk about themselves instead of about the listener?*
- *Are the supposed value statements clear and obviously beneficial to the listener?*
- *Does the talk constantly make the audience feel understood, respected, and appreciated?*
- *Can you sense humanity and personal connection that liven up data and statistics?*
- *Does the talk read like a shared personal value conversation or a typical product pitch?*
- *Is the speaker demonstrating passion for their work, values, and audience success?*
- *As a listener, are you inspired and motivated to take action?*
- *Is the call to action simple, immediate, and clear?*
- *Will the audience see how quick and easy it is to take their first or next step right away?*

Anything in your talk that does not put the audience front and center is hindering your message rather than helping it. Any moment where the value to them isn't obvious is the moment they begin to drift away and lose interest. Any statistic, metric, or data point that isn't brought to life by a personal story or proof of value is quickly forgotten.

Use your past presentations as a springboard to sharpen your future strategies. Learn from those times you failed one audience in order to deliver maximum value to the next audience. Dive back into your existing scripts as an exercise to add passion and create greater connection with the listener. Sometimes the fastest way to learn a new method is by building on an older, lesser method.

You Are in Very Good Company

If you've never considered this strategic planning approach to presentations before, you're not alone. Many of my top clients—highly paid executives and experts in their fields—have also never applied these types of pregame strategies. Like you, they get their assignment and just begin to write. Then they rewrite. Then re-rewrite some more, ad nauseam, right up to the moment of their talk, wasting countless hours and increasing their stress levels. And they still miss the value, passion, and connection they initially hoped to achieve. Starting with these questions will help you avoid that pitfall.

Even seasoned speakers tend to enter each new content creation process with too little focus on *why* they want to say what they want to say. They absent-mindedly place their own brands at the fore, expecting the audience to automatically feel the value for themselves. Ninety-nine times out of 100, passion is nowhere to be seen or heard. This is why most talks you've attended feel mediocre, why they meander and ultimately miss their mark.

I spend as much time coaching C-suite speakers on their content as I do on their delivery of that content. Why? Because weak content wastes time and is impossible to deliver well, and stronger content saves time and leads to better natural storytelling. Before you can practice any aspect of physical presentation (stance, command of the stage, facial expression, vocal inflection), you first have to know your content will support you from the first word of your talk to the last.

I like to ask my trainees to query their own reasons for delivering a talk in the first place. Many don't know; they're offered a keynote slot, and they take it. Together, we step back to assess their core value proposition, meaningful audience benefit, and clarity of purpose. Until these are addressed, scripts and slides have to wait. The results are eye opening; a stitch in time really does save nine, along with unnecessary hours of editing and miles of frayed nerves.

Anyone who commits to this early form of discovery will create differentiation from the vast majority of speakers who never bother to do so. Knowing *why* you choose to say *what* you choose to say fosters deep value and successful connection through understanding and delivering for your listener. And it all begins with pregame planning.

Slides and Graphics

Your slide deck requires the same clarity of purpose and focus on value. We'll delve deeper into visual corporate storytelling in later chapters, but the value-driven questions I describe above will apply to your screen as much as they do to your script.

Repeat the assessment exercise with a recent PowerPoint deck, either from the same talk or a totally different presentation. Start with slide one and assess each bullet point, image, and graphic with the same critical, audience-focused eye.

- *Are my slides clear and supportive, or confusing and distracting?*
- *Do I offer simple three- to five-word bullets, or complete sentences (or even paragraphs)?*
- *Are my slides giving subtle cues, or do they read like a complete script?*
- *Are my slides providing value for my audience, or just helping me remember what to say?*
- *Does what is on each of my slides enhance my content or compete with it?*
- *Do my slides say what I say, or require my audience to read and listen to different content simultaneously?*
- *Do my graphs and images tell a story, or do they just fill space for no reason?*
- *Do they tell my audience's story or my own company story?*
- *Is the value in each slide clear and compelling the moment it hits the screen?*

- ❑ *Can my audience instantly internalize each visual and quickly return to my storytelling?*
- ❑ *Do I highlight one primary value per slide, or bury value with too much content?*
- ❑ *Could my presentation deliver full value even if my slides suddenly crashed or vanished?*

I love that last one. Your slides are meant to enhance your talk, not compete with or overtake it. A favorite question I like to ask in coaching is, "If your slides tell the whole story, then why do we need you?" Any presentation that can just as easily be read off the screen, on a website, or in an email is a presentation that doesn't require a living, breathing human being to deliver it. The story has to come from you—your mouth, your heart, and your experience—not from your PowerPoint deck.

Each time you click to the next slide, you are deliberately ceding authority to your visuals. As soon as the graphic arrives, the audience leaves your face and directs their attention to the screen instead. Humans are visual creatures; we'll always see and read before we hear and listen. Make sure your slides are worth the diversion you create.

Just as you have in your scripted content, get it right up front. Ensuring each slide provides immediate and undeniable value for your viewers will save time-consuming redesign work down the road. Look at your slides objectively, from your audience's perspective, and ask, "Where will they find value in these graphics and bullets?" If you can't tell, neither will they. And if nothing gets sold until the story gets told, it follows that nothing gets sold until the story gets seen and read.

PAUL TRAYNOR

Documentary Filmmaker | Writer | Video Producer

I am drawn to politics for the stories, in the same way I'm drawn to Shakespeare, horror movies, and comic books. The stakes are high, life and death hang in the balance, and the very future of our planet, our people, and our global community teeters on the brink of potential annihilation. Who can resist such drama? To engage in political storytelling can be exhausting or de-moralizing but also rife with deep connection, the appearance of unexpected allies, and the possibility of changing lives and altering fate. An eternal struggle between good and evil.

Politics has always been built on storytelling to help us make sense of, and alter the course of, our world. Political stories are how we connect to daily life—and how life unfolds around us. Beginning. Middle. End. Three elemental compo-nents that describe every facet of being. Things were this way. Then something happened. Now it's like this.

These days, political rivalry is ratcheted up into stories that feel almost too dramatic. Heroes confronting villains; trickery, deception, and betrayal. Us versus Them. As divided Americans, we have wildly divergent views of the Beginning and little to no tolerance for alternate versions of the inevi-table End. The only thing we seem to agree upon is that it will be apocalyptic.

But still, the stories draw us, compel us, and challenge us to partake. "The Politics of Us" is the ultimate story, how we ascribe meaning to our own lives and realities—epic, spiritual, and mysterious. Because we don't remember the Beginning, and we can't see the End. We are perpetually trapped in the Middle, where the struggle and transformation occurs, where setbacks overwhelm us, and where the boon that might save and bless those we love waits in the next word or on the next page. We only get to decide whether to join the battle or to watch from the sidelines. Such wonderful drama.

CHAPTER FIVE

WHY ME? WHY IN PERSON? WHY THIS TALK?

THE MOST EFFECTIVE WAY OF ENSURING THAT YOUR TALK SAYS AND does what you want it to say and do is to clearly define your precise purpose in delivering it, along with your audience's precise purpose in attending it. You have to know why you are speaking in order to speak successfully. And you have to know what your audience is expecting to hear in order for them to truly hear anything you plan to say.

Remember, the audience always comes first, not you or your product. Their needs are the ones that really count, and fulfilling those needs is the only way to ensure ROI for your efforts and for your company. If you don't fully understand the exact goals and payoffs in your presentation, neither will they. And if you don't adhere closely to those goals and payoffs as you write and design your content, you're likely to go astray.

In order to achieve these important, time-saving targets, you have one more series of valuable preparation questions to ask yourself before diving into your script and slides.

Why Me?

Quiz yourself: "Why am I giving this talk?" Not "Why do I have to give it?" or "How can I get through it as quickly and with as little effort as possible?" You want to focus on why it has to be *you* in particular and not someone else in your department or organization. Why did the powers that be decide you should be the one to deliver this particular message to this particular audience? Again, if you don't know, neither will we.

You were trusted to carry this information to customers, partners, or analysts on behalf of your team. That is a serious honor and responsibility and deserves to be treated accordingly. Someone believes you bring something special to the topic, perhaps experience, credibility, or unique insight. Maybe it's your particular perspective or your proven relationships with customers or partners. Maybe you're the only one who had the time in your calendar. Not sure? Go find out. Discover who suggested you, and ask them the "Why me?" question.

Whatever the reasons you were chosen, embrace them, accept them, and use them to your advantage. Include those perspectives and relationships in the opening welcome to your talk as an effective tool for establishing trust and respect with your listeners. If your boss wanted you to tackle this topic, let your audience know:

> My team wanted me to share our story with you because this is my passion and my favorite thing to talk about with friends and colleagues like you. I love showing what we've built and how it pays off for our partners and customers—so you're in excellent hands!

Share why you are the perfect person to be up on that stage as a representative of your brand. Tell your audience precisely why your voice is the one that will make a difference in their lives and how lucky they are to have you as their session guide.

Why in Person?

Ask yourself: "Why does this presentation need to be given by a human being?" In other words, what is it about this content that must be presented live, face-to-face, in a dedicated room, at great expense, requiring the investment of everyone's time and energy? Why couldn't this particular message be delivered in print instead, or through an email blast or micro-site? If it could, then the audience has no need for you.

If your story is nothing more than simple regurgitation of data, copied and pasted from the company website or product manual, the hard truth is that there is no compelling reason for your talk to be delivered in person. Your audi-ence will be served just as well or even better by reading your content for them-selves, on their own time and dime, when it's more convenient and applicable.

Honest assessment of the purpose and goals of your presentation re-quires accepting that success and value don't come solely from information, but from the personal story you bring to that information. If it's not per-sonal, it's strictly informational. And that's not a talk, it's a manual, a lecture rather than a conversation. The only reason for you to give any public talk is *you*—*your* views, *your* experiences, and *your* values. Without those, we'd be just as happy scanning through a white paper in the comfort of our homes.

Why This Talk?

One of my favorite questions to ask in coaching is "What percentage of your content do you think the audience will remember an hour af-ter you've finished speaking?" Most responses are exceedingly optimistic, maybe 30%–50%. Some give a pessimistic guess of 10%–20%. In truth, even the pessimists are optimists. Multiple models, from Dale's Cone of Experience[12] to Miller's Magic Number[13] to Craik and Lockhart's Levels of Processing[14] suggest that, after a few hours or days, your audience will recall as little as 3%–8% of what you tell them during your talk. Unsurprisingly, this harsh reality is unwelcome news for most speakers.

---

12 Lee, Sang Joon, and Thomas C. Reeves. "Edgar Dale and the Cone of Experience." In *Foundations of Learning and Instructional Design Technology*, edited by Richard E West. Pressbooks, 2018. https://www.lidtfoundations.pressbooks.com/chapter/edgar-dale-and-the-cone-of-experience/.

13 Cowan, Nelson. "George Miller's Magical Number of Immediate Memory in Retrospect: Observations on the Faltering Progression of Science." *Psychological Review* 122, no. 3 (2015): 536–41. https://www.ncbi.nlm.nih.gov/pmc/articles/PMC4486516/.

14 McLeod, Saul. "Levels of Processing." Simply Psychology. December 2007. https://www.simplypsychology.org/levelsofprocessing.html.

Some find it demoralizing: "Why bother if most of my talk is ultimately forgotten?" Some are confident that *their* talk will be the outlier, the one session strong enough to overcome the science. And, to be fair, many studies on memory and recollection are highly controversial since they rely on a wide range of subjective variances that do, in fact, accidentally move the numbers up or down. Let's assume your talk has considered all those variables and will rise to the top on its own merits. You've ensured deep value, crafted expert storytelling, built supportive visuals, and added meaningful personal insights that ignite a connection with your listeners. You still have one more hurdle to clear: the event calendar.

If your talk is scheduled at the start of a full conference day, your audience may still be waking up and not at peak capacity for absorbing data. Even if they are wide awake and ready to lean in, they may eagerly soak up your talk only to have it slowly pushed from their minds over the next seven hours of heavily loaded session content. We're only human, and the smartest and most attentive viewer can only recall so much information in the next hour or by the next day. It's not personal. Despite your audience's best intentions, most of your content will be subconsciously and unintentionally sacrificed as the hours tick past. Given this reality, 3%–8% retention of your talk is not so bad, and shouldn't be surprising.

Perhaps your session is scheduled at the end of a full conference day, the last of eight long hours that have been packed with dozens of speakers and back-to-back presentations. By the time your talk arrives, your audience may already be mentally and, perhaps, physically exhausted. They're tired and hungry, with 200 unopened emails and multiple voicemails and requests from home and office to respond to. Your content is the only thing standing between them and a glass of wine. If that audience can internalize and recall 3%–8% of your content, it's a big win.

Adding to those challenges are the multitude of modern technologies constantly vying for your audience's attention as you speak. When Dale, Miller, and Craik and Lockhart were doing their research on memory and retention (1946, 1956, 1972), they weren't accounting for social media and instant messaging. Now we have a portable computer in our hands

24/7/365, commanding our slavish loyalty. By today's standards, when everyone in our audience is a frenetic multitasker, 3%–8% recollection of any talk is quite impressive.

All these considerations point to the most important question you can ask yourself about the content you plan to include in your talk: "If my audience will only remember 3%–8% of my content, what should that 3%–8% be?" When speakers ask me why any talk is worth giving if over 90% of it will be forgotten in a matter of minutes or days, I help them recognize why this limited recollection is actually empowering rather than disappointing.

All speakers can tell you what their key takeaways are, but few speakers address those key takeaways as the only things their attendees are likely to walk away with. A confident focus on the most vital 3%–8% of your content, those two or three great ideas that connect with and inspire your viewers, lets you happily sacrifice the unimportant so the important can speak louder and create more human connection. A narrow memory lens takes pressure off you as the speaker, allowing you to focus on what matters most to your attendees. And because your audience won't remember most of your talk's deep dive details, you can replace some of those endless data points and statistical complexities with more personal passion and listener value.

Remember, your goal is to be motivational more than you are informational. Let the cream of your talk rise to the top and get you into each viewer's *high-value* bin. Then, next week, when your audience is back in their offices, recalling the best topics from the conference, your 3%–8% will stand out and compel them to action.

Why Planning Pays Off

Dale's Cone of Experience posited that the least effective method of message retention is one-way learning from information presented through verbal symbols (i.e., listening to spoken words). The most effective method of message retention involves what we now call "experiential learning" or "action learning," suggesting we incorporate and gain more value from what we *do* as opposed to what we *hear*, *read*, or *observe*. Our job as speakers is to pull all these stimuli together, offering both spoken words *and* action learning in our talks in a way that maximizes potential for message memory.

Motivating your listeners will ensure they observe and absorb your presentation then take action on it; this is the "doing" part of their experience. The speed of that action is paramount. With only 3%–8% of your talk in their minds and a short memory cycle to compete with, you want to motivate your audience to act on that minimal content takeaway as quickly as possible, before it begins to erode or get transported to their *low-value* bins.

A speaker should always conclude every talk with a specific and immediate ask. We refer to this important last salvo as the "call to action." In Chapter Eight, we will dive into how to create a successful call to action at the conclusion of your talk.

I am always surprised by how many speakers neglect to offer a strong call to action before thanking their audience and leaving the spotlight. They run out of slides, and they run away, a regrettable fumble that fails to capitalize on a successful session or set up a next point of contact. Other speakers might include a call to action but give it short shrift, nothing more than a perfunctory invitation to visit a URL, download a report, or call to learn more. These asks are as worthless as no call to action at all.

As you prepare to begin drafting your next talk, consider that everything you are about to write should point both back to your strong opening title and forward toward your confident, prescriptive call to action. Ask yourself three more questions:

1   *What specific action do I want my audience to take the moment my talk ends and why?*

2   *How can I get them to take that action right away instead of waiting?*

3   *How will I ensure that action will help them achieve instant, positive results?*

The goal of your presentation is always to deliver value and benefit for your attendees. When you start your content creation process knowing exactly where it should end, how every part of your story reveals the 3%–8% that matters most, and what is most likely to motivate viewers to immediate proactivity, you save tons of preparation time, and your odds of success will soar.

Lead with Learning Objectives

When I coach a speaker, I always put extra focus on the intended key takeaways of their upcoming talk. Most of the time, those takeaways miss the target. Here are the learning objectives I hear most often:

> *"I want them to see how great our product is, and then I want them to buy it."*
>
> *"They should go download our software and learn how to use it."*
>
> *"We want them to get excited enough to set up a site visit."*
>
> *"Once they see how much better our service is, they'll click the URL to learn more."*
>
> *"If I show them how other companies use our solution, they'll see how to use it too."*

Can you hear the problem? Learning objectives should be for the audience, not for the speaker. Most speakers do not understand this vital distinction and focus on key takeaways that fit their own priorities and desires rather than those of their attendees. This mistake leads those speakers to write a script and design slides with the wrong intent, resulting in a weak story with little chance the audience will invest or take action.

You may want the audience to buy your product, learn to use your software, set up a site visit, or click the URL, but those intentions serve *your* interests, not your viewers'. Your audience will know they aren't the priority. Turn your learning objectives outward toward your listeners instead, and those objectives will guide you toward a stronger story that nets the response you seek.

For each learning objective you hope to deliver, adapt that takeaway to make it about the viewer instead of about you. For example:

"Understand the power of our software, then download and learn how to use it."

Turns into

"Empower your team by cutting mean time to resolution by 70% in just five minutes."

"Get excited about partnering with us and set up a site visit."

Turns into

"Deliver better user experiences and improve your customer retention rates."

"Show how we digitized our network and achieved better results."

Turns into

"Show how easily you can digitize your network for less cost and faster turnaround times."

Edit your learning objectives to deliver value and benefit for your guests. Those crystal clear objectives then serve as your launchpad for everything that follows, a shining point of reference to justify each word in your script and each bullet on your slides.

MICHELLE JUEHRING

Race Director | Marketing Executive | Ironman Triathlete

As a race director and self-described "back of the pack" endurance athlete, I have found that telling stories does far more than make the miles go by faster; it strengthens the human spirit and deepens both personal and professional connections.

To date, I've run 26 races—a mix of marathons, 10Ks, and 5Ks. I've participated in three century rides and completed an Ironman triathlon. All these commitments required countless hours of training and conditioning and challenges to the body and mind demanding fortitude and uncommon perseverance. To survive and surpass, we athletes rely on stories that give us strength and light the trail ahead.

My workout partners and I often hit those trails in the early morning hours, up before the sun, partners in accountability, encouragement, and follow-through. We tell stories to pass the time and to keep each other motivated. These "marathon stories" might normally take 30 seconds to tell, but stretched out over half a mile, they push us, step-by-step, and reveal far more than the stories themselves. Spirits rise and friendships are formed as we tell our tales and tick off another day of training.

One woman stoically endured the searing Midwest heat in July as her husband served in Desert Storm. Another walked circles on her driveway for hours on end through the pandemic, preparing for her next race. These wonderful souls and powerful athletes don't just compete; they understand *why* they feel compelled to push beyond their own limits. They know their own passions and generously offer to share those passions with others.

As the director of a world-class seven-mile race,[15] I'm in a position of remarkable privilege to hear so many passionate, inspiring, and motivating stories of why people run. Great stories lead to great human connections, weaving together the fabric of our souls, building authentic relationships, and paving mutual roads to victory.

---

15   http://bix7.com.

CHAPTER SIX

YOUR TITLE IS YOUR PROMISE

WITH YOUR LEARNING OBJECTIVES CLEARLY DEFINED AND POINT-
ing you toward a value-driven presentation, it's time to begin enticing people with the talk you eventually plan to deliver. Proving value in your talk
begins long before you step on stage or go on camera. Your commitment to
an audience kicks off weeks or even months in advance, at the point when
you first ask them to set aside future time in their calendars in order to attend your talk. It's a big ask, which requires a big payoff.

The title and abstract you submit in proposal for your topic have several tasks to accomplish, beginning with getting your talk selected for inclusion at an event or conference. While most speakers choose a title that's
highly clinical and obvious, a little effort in this opening point of contact
can and should achieve so much more. As I say in my coaching programs,
your title is vital.

The title of your talk is an offer of value on which you promise to
deliver. It is your proposition that if someone (wisely) chooses to attend
your talk, perhaps even over someone else's, they are guaranteed to receive
a specific set of tangible benefits that warrant their investment in you.

If your talk is going to be part of a larger conference or symposium,
your title is also a promise to the event selection committee that they
should add your topic to their program instead of another competing sub-
mission. You owe that committee the best possible session because it will

ultimately reflect on them as much as it does on you.

Too many speakers submit a proposed talk, get selected, then move it to the back burner until the last minute. That is unfair and unprofessional. The moment your session is included, it deserves your full attention and a commitment to excellence. You made a promise of value that you are now responsible for fulfilling. Only submit a title you actually *want* to deliver, one you are proud of and excited to share. Anything less undervalues you as a speaker, disrespects the time and dedication of your audience, and abuses the trust bestowed on you by your event hosts. And it all starts with your session title.

Most talks settle for basic, straightforward titles that are obvious, unimaginative, and uninspiring:

"Middleprise Mobile Backhaul and Fronthaul Evolution"

"Distributed Ledger Technology: Transforming Credentialing"

"A Bold, New Network for Infrastructure and Application Developers"

These titles are too on the nose, too flat, and too corporate to make any meaningful promise or personal connection with a potential attendee. The audience may choose to attend if the topic speaks directly to their area of specialty, but they will enter the room in a few weeks or months not knowing what to expect or what (if any) value they are going to receive. Even if a boring title suggests it covers information that the attendee needs to learn, they have been given no sense of what the speaker is actually offering, what level of expertise is required, or if the content is directed at their specific needs. Titles like these read as peer-reviewed term paper proposals rather than value commitments.

On the other hand, sometimes titles get a bit too creative:

"Fear and Loathing in Cybersecurity: An Analysis of the Psychology of Cloud Terror"

"Are You Playing a Game of Jeopardy with Your Contracts?"

"From Travel Hell to Travel Well"

While these titles tell us even less about the talk than our previous examples, they at least attempt to make us feel something. We still don't know exactly what we'll learn during these sessions, and they still lack specific value propositions despite their clever attempts at attention grabs. As these speakers got more creative, their titles lost the plot. While there can be value in a sense of humor or flair for the dramatic, neither will matter if the payoff for the intended audience remains a mystery.

Here are some titles that deliver both sides of the promise. These provide good opening stories that also bring the speaker's value into clear focus:

"New Methods of Connecting with Your Clients for Mutual Business Success"

"Three Proven Ways to Increase Patient Results Using Cool and Affordable Technologies"

"How Small Distribution Centers Can Deliver More and Spend Less"

Where most titles underperform and lack clarity, each of these examples inspires and entices in one single, easily understandable line of text. Each example succeeds in five measurable metrics:

1. A strong title *promises the audience a valuable benefit*. We know exactly what we're going to learn in the talk and why we need to learn it, and it's clear that the talk will hold real value for us.
2. A strong title *tells a story*. Instead of simply labeling a solution or service, we get a compelling picture of why it matters and how it will make a positive, meaningful difference in our lives.
3. A strong title *makes us curious*. The title pulls us into the narrative and sparks anticipation before we enter the room. We're already

thinking, "Yes, that's exactly what I want for myself and for my organization!"

4. A strong title *gives us FOMO*. Fear of missing out is a powerful motivator. If we don't attend this talk, our competition might get a benefit that we won't. We have to be in that room.

5. A strong title *becomes a guide for content creation*. The right title serves as a powerful beacon for the presenter once they begin to write and rehearse their talk, a guardrail to ensure each word and graphic serves the title's promise to the viewer.

In my coaching workshops, I ask participants to help craft a powerful session title for a talk they have never given. You can try this exercise as well. Imagine you are preparing for a new presentation on 5G technology at an upcoming wireless distribution technology summit. You want to offer your conference a strong, engaging title to convince event coordinators to select your talk and to ensure attendees are eager to add you to their session calendars. Here's your premise:

> For years, we've been hearing about the potential speed and strength of 5G, but it still feels more like a dream than a reality. The struggle to deliver 5G persists as every key player prioritizes their own agenda. Mistrust and proprietary control create competition rather than partnership in bringing 5G to fruition. Device manufacturers, antenna installers, service providers, building owners, and jurisdictional authorities must join forces for a better global communications future. Cooperation is the only practical path to a comprehensive 5G reality.

You have a good story that now needs a good title. You want to create one connective line that sums up this topic and tells your audience exactly what value promise they can expect if they choose to attend your session. Start by writing a basic, no-nonsense, strictly technical title. Make it as long or short as you like, but stick to the facts, and keep it utilitarian. There should be no personality, flash, or creativity.

Title 1: _____

Now read your simple, no-frills title from the perspective of an attendee at the conference. As you scan the titles of dozens or hundreds of breakout options on offer during that event, how likely are you to choose that particular title and add it to your show calendar? Is it clear what immediate value awaits you in this session? Does the title excite and motivate you? Or would you rather hold out for a more compelling, higher-value title during the same time slot?

Go back and reread the abstract. Now craft a second, purely creative title. This time, focus less on your technology and more on capturing an audience's attention through fun or surprise. You can be clever or ominous or use any other creative approach that makes this more dramatic title stand out and begin to tell a story. Let your imagination take over.

Title 2: _____

Once again, try to analyze your more creative title from an outside perspective. Read it as if for the first time, with no idea who the speaker is or what their talk will contain. Is this title more or less likely to hook you as an attendee than the previous, dry title? Does it pull you in or turn you off? Are you intrigued or confused? Even if this second title is snappier, there's probably still not enough to go on. It may be cute or funny or intriguing, but it's probably not very concrete. Maybe this title suggests the speaker is entertaining, but you're not choosing this talk just to be entertained; you're here to learn and to achieve actionable benefits. If you can't easily see the value promise in this title, will you still attend?

Reread the abstract one more time, then try crafting a title that brings both sides of the coin—informative and creative—together. Combine fact and story into a compelling line that turns your talk into a million-dollar promise. Remember the measurable metrics your title should offer to your audience:

1. Promise a benefit. We see exactly what we'll learn and what value to expect.
2. Tell a story. Your topic is clear and compelling enough for anyone to feel a part of.
3. Make us curious. The title pulls us in and makes us want to hear more.
4. Give us FOMO. If we don't attend your talk, we are missing out on something important.

We'll get back to metric five in a moment, but try to include at least two of these elements as you write your strong 5G title.

Title 3: _____

Once more, imagine yourself as an attendee at this conference. Read your new title and ask yourself if this is the exact value you've been looking for in the event session listings. Does it directly address your current need and compel you to learn more? Does it give you a sense of the speaker, who they are, and why they care about delivering this talk? Do you clearly recognize why you should add it to your event calendar?

This exercise is valuable because it helps you to discover what your core content should be and acts as a North Star for how to construct your talk. Crafting a great title sharpens the promise you're making to your audience and the decisive intent you carry into your session. Now that you've tried this exercise on your own titles, let's do a similar analysis of someone else's titles based on those metrics.

One of these 5G talk titles meets the key criteria we've discussed above, and the other does not. On first read, which feels more successful?

A. "Working Together to Turn 5G Cellular from a Dream into a Reality"

B. "Partnership and Trust in 5G: Meeting Global Demand by Raising All Boats for All Players"

Let's break them down using our first four metrics to see how they compare:

1. A strong title *promises the audience a valuable benefit.* We know exactly what we're going to learn in the talk and why we need to learn it, and it's clear that the talk will hold real value for us.

Title A suggests a worthy goal and the final target we all hope to reach, but it doesn't explain what we'll learn during the talk. We know we have to work together to make 5G a reality, but if it's that easy, then why hasn't it already happened? There is no proposed solution promised.

Title B sets up a premise of partnership and trust, something we know is lacking in today's path to 5G. It also promises we'll learn how to meet global demand by raising all boats together instead of continuing to work at odds with one another.

2. A strong title *tells a story.* Instead of just labeling a solution or service, we get a compelling picture of why it matters and how it will make a positive, meaningful difference in our lives.

Title A is an optimistic view of our industry, but while it consolidates the core concept of our topic, it doesn't tell much of a story to compel attendance. This title feels more like a pitch and less like a vision of a better future.

Title B addresses all players in the room and tells an energized, confident story that creates an imperative for our industry. It almost dares us to take part or get left behind.

3. A strong title *makes us curious.* The title pulls us into the narrative and sparks anticipation before we enter the room. We're already thinking, "Yes, that's exactly what I want for myself and for my organization!"

Title A restates the frustration we've all felt for years as we wait on a long-promised 5G future. We know we want to see that future as soon as possible, but this title doesn't say how we'll do things differently than we have up until now. It doesn't make us curious.

Title B challenges us to think and work differently, with trust rather than skepticism, for the benefit of all global citizens rather than purely for our own profit. We're suddenly curious as to how to make this cooperation happen, and we need to hear more.

4. *A strong title gives us FOMO.* Fear of missing out is a powerful motivator. If we don't attend this talk, our competition might get a benefit that we won't. We have to be in that room.

Title A is utilitarian and straightforward but not quite compelling. If we miss this talk, there will be plenty of others like it to come. While the title sounds optimistic, it feels a bit "been there, done that, didn't work." It doesn't propose a real change in the status quo. No FOMO.

Title B is bold and confident, suggesting a unique, new approach to solving our shared problem, one we have to hear, understand, and be a part of. If the other players in our industry know how to build that trust, and we don't, we could be left out of the equation; we can't risk missing out on fresh methods of partnership. Successful FOMO.

Now that we know how to recognize a strong title versus a weak title, let's reintroduce the fifth measurable metric.

5. A strong title *becomes a guide for content creation.* The right title serves as a powerful beacon for the presenter once they begin to write and rehearse their talk, a guardrail to ensure each word and graphic serves the title's promise to the viewer.

This goal initially supports the speaker, then ultimately serves the audience. A strong title sets up your topic, hones your delivery goals, and becomes your powerful scripting and designing partner, pointing you toward fulfilling the specific promise you've made. The right title makes your content creation job easier, setting you up for success and increasing the likelihood of a satisfying payoff for your viewers.

In contrast, a weak title can prevent you from delivering on your promise at all. Titles that promise the wrong thing or mislead attendees and event planners are a recipe for disaster and disappointment. Long before the talk takes place, a bad title can get any speaker into trouble. I call this "chasing the wrong rabbit down the wrong hole," and it has proven to be as good a lesson as any in my own content scripting and public speaking.

Let's measure our two 5G talk titles once more. Again, one meets the key target criterion for metric five, and the other does not. As the speaker setting out to craft this talk, how will each of these titles either guide you toward successful scripted content or confuse you through lack of clarity or vague intent?

A. "Working Together to Turn 5G Cellular from a Dream into a Reality"

Title A doesn't give you much to work with because it doesn't really offer any promise to your viewers. Without a story your attendees can relate to, they are less likely to be curious or to prioritize your session. With this title as your North Star, guiding everything that follows, whatever you write or design could easily be too generic, corporate, or data driven. The wrong North Star can leave you wandering alone and starving in the presentation desert.

B. "Partnership and Trust in 5G: Meeting Global Demand by Raising All Boats for All Players"

Title B sets a much stronger tone and demands more intent and inspiration. Because this title centers on trust and partnership, it keeps your content focused on the needs of the many rather than the self-serving few. The 5G future reflected in this title insists you write and design your corporate story from a more global, comprehensive perspective, one with a stronger chance of paying off for your audience.

Next, consider your title from the event planner's perspective. Event organizers sort through piles of abstracts, hoping to build an impressive and dynamic program offering numerous paths to success for their attendees. The titles these teams select are part of a mandate to excite and inspire more advance registrations and increase anticipation. Your title—and the talk that follows—helps determine the quality of their overall programming. Positive or negative reviews of your session have a direct impact on their jobs, their evaluations, and possibly even their paychecks. Your title carries a promise to these event leaders that your talk will make them look good by association. Titles and talks that receive weak surveys make that team look bad. Being a better team player begins with giving them a great title, then making sure that title pays off.

Metric five becomes the foundation for creating your entire talk, acting as a persistent "Bat-Signal" from the first word of your script to the last. Each line and slide are measured against your title's promise; if anything doesn't reflect that opening value proposition, out it goes.

Most conferences offer two to four concurrent breakouts in any given time slot to ensure a wide choice for their guests. Your talk's title could sway an attendee toward your session or toward a competing, simultaneous session. Is your title strong enough to win that battle? Does it deserve to win? If you're not sure, try writing multiple title options until you find the one that will. Sometimes finding out what you *don't* want to say is as valuable as discovering what you *do* want to say.

Craft a compelling story that viewers will be inspired by and excited for. Get them curious to learn more. Offer something they can't afford to miss. Ensure you can deliver what your attendees actually want and need to hear. Take time and care with your talk's title, and your room will be full while others in your time slot face empty seats.

Your Abstract Expands on Your Promise

If your title is the first line of a compelling story, your abstract then kicks that story into high gear, ramping up the intensity and hooking us with your key characters and exciting plotline. A great abstract is your argument for buy-in, enticing potential attendees with all the reasons why your talk will be well worth their priority, time, and investment. Strong abstracts are constructed on three important strategies:

1. *One-hundred percent focus on the attendee* and the specific ways your talk will challenge them, inspire them, and pay off for them. If your abstract is about you, your product, or your success, redirect it to tell the audience's story instead. Change "we," "our," and "they" to "you," "your," and "us." The more personal you make your abstract, the more personally your audience will feel it and connect with it.

2. *Nothing but value and positive results* from beginning to end. Abstracts that ramble or get caught up in technical detail and corporate speak do nothing for an intended viewer. Don't save your big value payoffs for two-thirds of the way down your abstract; lead with them. Ask questions that address core challenges, followed by unambiguous promises of how you'll solve those challenges to make a powerful and immediate difference. Every word in your abstract should be a flashing arrow pointing to VALUE, VALUE, VALUE!!!

3. *Create FOMO for the audience.* Your abstract should subtly say to the reader, "You can't afford to miss my talk. If your competitor shows up but you don't, they'll get this information, and you won't." Without being overly aggressive, think of your abstract as tantamount to daring them not to hear about the benefits you'll provide.

Let's read a sample abstract to see if it achieves these three strategic targets. Like all content, this is subjective; some will see an abstract as successful, while others will think it misses the mark:

In the wake of new privacy regulations, companies are being forced to evaluate their privacy practices and comply with hundreds of data protection requirements. This session will teach attendees how to gain efficiencies by leveraging the NIST Privacy Framework to evaluate their privacy capabilities, align to applicable regulations, and streamline privacy compliance in one place.

Not only does this abstract not maintain 100% focus on the attendee, it actually puts zero focus on the attendee. We get words like "companies," "attendees," and "their," third-party entities we don't know or care about; these are easily changed to "your company," "you/your," and "our." While an expert in the field may see some value in this pitch, the corporate speak completely suppresses any inspiration, motivation, or excitement on offer. For example, "gain efficiencies" is a weak substitute for "your team can work more efficiently," and "privacy capabilities" should be "understanding your levels of privacy." Regarding FOMO, this doesn't give me any. If I miss this talk, there will be dozens more like it down the road. If my competition attends, and I don't, I'm not so worried.

Let's try a quick rework to bring out the better story buried in this abstract:

Constantly growing and changing privacy regulations are forcing all of us to evaluate our privacy practices and comply with hundreds of data protection requirements. You're looking for more efficiency and a genuine, real-time understanding of how privacy works in your organization right now. I'll show you how to leverage the NIST Privacy Framework to know exactly how well your privacy is protecting you and your end users. And I'll show you how it can work so much better. In 30 minutes, you'll recognize how to align your business to

> any applicable regulation and how to start streamlining your privacy compliance in one place.

Can you hear how those small changes net big results? Here's another abstract for us to put through the same critical assessment:

> Would you like to know more about cooling tower water treatment? "Water Treatment Fundamentals" will provide an overview of the basics of water treatment for evaporative heat rejection equipment, including open-circuit and closed-circuit cooling towers as well as evaporative condensers. Topics to be covered include common water treatment terms, methods for control of scale, corrosion, and biological contamination, water-management plans, and best practices for minimizing water use while maximizing system efficiency.

100% focus on the attendee? Not so much. There's a single use of "you" in the first sentence, and I do appreciate the opening question, but there's nothing else to make this abstract personal; it's just a dull grocery list of subjects to be covered. While there may be some value in these topics, the abstract is clinical and academic, difficult to get excited about. There's certainly not much FOMO here—just another technical talk that doesn't elevate itself or create an expectation of learning something special.

Let's take a crack at revising this abstract for more impact:

> Have you ever wanted to know the ins and outs of cooling tower water treatment? If not, you should! Water treatment fundamentals affect every aspect of your operation and efficiency.

> I'm going to give you a valuable crash course in the basics of
> water treatment so you have complete understanding of your
> evaporative heat rejection equipment, open-circuit and closed-
> circuit cooling towers, and evaporative condensers. You'll learn
> all the common water treatment terms, as well as methods you
> can use to control scale, corrosion, and biological contamination.
> We'll check out winning water-management plans. And you'll
> walk away with a new set of best practices for minimizing water
> use while maximizing system efficiency.

A little redirection and adherence to our three key success targets can turn any pedestrian, underperforming abstract into a valuable, passionate, connective opening to your corporate story. Let's look at one more example:

> Reining in your supply chain challenges is like herding cats.
> You have to reimagine fulfillment, move faster, and be more
> efficient. This means your warehouses and distribution centers
> need more storage, better throughput, and new-age robotics.
> This talk will get you there, quickly and at scale. Get ready for
> smarter infrastructure investments that prioritize your agility
> and give you more bang for the buck. Discover how to use
> affordable, accessible, predictive artificial intelligence that serves
> your customers and maintains a steady flow of goods-to-person
> processes. A few wise and wonderful upgrades will keep your
> organization on top and more aligned for today's and tomorrow's
> growing supply chain demands. See you there!

Now we're talking. This speaker successfully keeps their abstract 100% focused on the attendee, directly addressing their current needs and end goals. They understand what we want to hear and how to move us toward success. We get value from the first word to the last, with something enticing and inspiring in each sentence. This talk is what we've been waiting for. This abstract definitely gives us FOMO; we have to learn these tips and tricks in order to maintain market share, and we can't afford to pass up this opportunity. Well done.

Your title is your promise of value and payoff to your guests, your event coordinators, and yourself. As the opening line of your eventual corporate story, the right title sets everyone off on a quest for benefit and success. Then your abstract picks up where the title leaves off, building on your story's opening line to introduce your characters, plot, and anticipation of the journey ahead.

Remember, your title and abstract are designed for your viewers first and foremost. Tell them what they want and need to hear, and you'll attract them to your presentation. The earlier you can excite guests to join your session, the more opportunities you will have to reach a wider and more enthusiastic audience.

Chief Marketing Officer | Franchise Executive | Creative Strategist

Years ago, as a newly minted account executive at Leo Burnett, I pitched Quangles multigrain chips using the well-known Dr. Seuss story, *Green Eggs and Ham*. Consumer research indicated that heavy snackers wouldn't love the idea of a multigrain chip, so we likened the challenge to Sam-I-Am's; instead of PowerPoint slides, I gave a dramatic reading leading up to the story's climactic moment: "I do so like a Quangles chip!" We sold the strategy because we sold a familiar, recognizable, and personally meaningful story.

The most memorable and persuasive advertising has always come in the form of a good story. Amazon's commercial about a priest and an imam exchanging gifts was a touching, tangible demonstration of common value. Volkswagen's commercial about a boy dressed as Darth Vader humanized the product in a way that product's attributes or statistical benefits could never have done.

Technology has made it easier for anyone to create shallow, point-and-click advertising for a distracted and oversaturated marketplace. Why bother with a story when you can just play the numbers, convincing one consumer out of millions to click a little ad on their phone and initiate an immediate transaction? That strategy may find temporary success at a low price point, but lasting customer relationships and meaningful investments come from telling the right story.

The right story is built on authenticity and shared experiences—an honest connection that attracts an honest response. Genuine introspection, careful thought, and emotional storytelling will always pay off. And they make selling chips—or anything else—a whole lot more fun.

CHAPTER SEVEN

CREATING THICKNESS

You recognize why nothing gets sold until the story gets told. You understand your audience and what they want and need to hear from you. You realize the core value you hope to deliver with your presentation. You have a strategy for making that value more personal and less corporate. You know what you're passionate about and how to bring that passion to the fore of your topic. And you've created a strong title from which to build your story. It's time to start crafting your upcoming talk.

One of my favorite coaching concepts centers on what I call "thick versus thin" presentations. Thick presentations are like a great sandwich: layered, meaty, packed with texture, and satisfying for an audience to consume. They leave the viewer full and happy. Thin presentations—the usual fare we encounter at conferences and sales meetings—are unfulfilling and forgettable. They lack flavor and complexity, leaving us uninspired and wishing we'd ordered something else.

We can also apply a home builder analogy. Have you ever been in a "thin" house? It feels cheap the moment you walk through the door, thrown together, rushed, and flimsy. You instantly sense that corners were cut through lack of investment: walls with scant insulation, uneven floors, and misaligned windows. The plumbing rattles, and the fixtures leak; the house is clearly not built to last. It's nothing more than another "get in, get out" cookie cutter designed for rapid turnover. Whoever buys it won't pay much, and their investment won't be secure.

The metaphor is obvious. If your talk is nothing but selling products, laden with cut-and-paste pitch points, awash in readily available metrics, it's thin. If your talk also includes humanity, personal perspective, connectivity, and audience-driven value, it's thick. You've built something substantial that any buyer will be eager to invest in.

Unfortunately, thin presentations are the norm, and are easy to spot from the first words out of a speaker's mouth. The audience enters a session with an uninspiring title or abstract and no real grasp of the speaker's approach, or whether they'll walk away with any meaningful value to take action on. The presenter steps onstage, introduces themselves, restates the name of the session, and runs through the agenda, and they're off into a dull series of energy-sapping PowerPoint slides. Once those slides run out, so does the speaker. It's all too clear that this was a minimal-effort presentation, hastily conceived, ill prepared, and with no thought for anything beyond fulfilling a job demand or meeting a sales quota. It's a thin talk that nets a thin response.

Sadly, many of us spend our careers giving these kinds of thin talks. One reason is that a thin talk is our easiest and most obvious path to easy project completion. Another reason is that it's a default form of self-sabotage that keeps the bar low and manages expectations: "I'm a weak speaker. I'm too busy anyway. It's their fault if I give a weak performance. Next time they'll know better and ask someone else." Between glossophobic aversion to public speaking and a desire to just get it over with, what point is there in making our talks thicker?

Still, we all want our talk to succeed, if for no other reason than that we want to look good in front of our peers and leadership. And we realize that a successful talk requires proving some quantity of tangible value for an audience. Delivering this value does not always require natural charm or impressive communication skills. You can conquer your self-sabotage by adding layers of humanity and storytelling into your talk for the benefit of your viewers. That thicker content will help convey the value you want to share, instantly making you a better public speaker by leveraging your inherent storytelling ability.

While you might not recognize or accept it yet, you already possess an innate evolutionary aptitude for telling a meaningful, connective, passionate story in service of another person. We'll fully address this organic aptitude, known as orality, in Chapter Ten. Because thickness adds value for both you and your listener, it helps you push through your layers of glossophobia, establishing trust and credibility. How can they judge you when you're giving them so much value and such obvious commitment to their future success?

Step 1: Thin Versus Thick

Instead of verbal analogies, let's present this thin-versus-thick concept in graphical terms. Here is a typical thin presentation structure, standard fare in the vast majority of talks we suffer through—or deliver ourselves:

- ❏ *Technical title*
- ❏ *Qualifying subtitle*
- ❏ *Name and job description*
- ❏ *Top industry challenges*
- ❏ *Introduce and explain product or solution one*
- ❏ *Introduce and explain product or solution two*
- ❏ *Introduce and explain product or solution three*
- ❏ *Thank you*

This thin approach gets the basic job done. It covers only what the boss or team expects and no more. It is easy to write, easy to learn, and easy to deliver, asking very little of the speaker or audience. Technically, everything is included, but it's a sterile and overly-corporate approach with no passion or personality to invest in or care about. Viewers have no sense of the most important 3%–8% they should recall once the speaker has left the stage; they may hear this talk, but they're unlikely to remember any of it or take action on its content.

Thin presentations only swim in the safe, shallow, sales-focused end of the pool where there's no depth, no risk, no excitement, and no skill required. This thin talk is a lecture, quickly thrown together and just as quickly forgotten. It might just as well be read off a screen.

Here is a thick presentation structure, laden with value and delivered in the same total amount of time:

- ❏ *Compelling title*
- ❏ *Clear value proposition*
- ❏ *The moment before*
- ❏ *Establish the why*
- ❏ *Personal experience*
- ❏ *Deeper meaning*
- ❏ *Agenda as a promise*
- ❏ *Challenge one / solution one*
- ❏ *Immediate value of result*
- ❏ *Proof of value*
- ❏ *Challenge two / solution two*
- ❏ *Immediate value of result*
- ❏ *Proof of value*
- ❏ *Challenge three / solution three*
- ❏ *Immediate value of result*
- ❏ *Proof of value*
- ❏ *Restatement of key values*
- ❏ *Agenda complete*
- ❏ *Strong call to action*
- ❏ *Genuine conclusion*

Even on paper, the difference is clear and compelling. All layers are present, and the story is far more complete and satisfying. From the outset, the audience is given the opportunity for connection and engagement. Before any information or data come into play, clear value lays the foundation for a strong ROI. A vision of success is first painted in the viewer's mind, so by the time the data and statistical core content arrive, the audience is leaning in, engaged, and understands exactly how those metrics will personally benefit their lives and businesses. Thick presentations respect the audience, motivate them, and instill confidence.

Despite the number of steps in each of these structures, both talks can be delivered in the same time frame and cover the same information. Adding layers doesn't mean adding minutes; it means giving fewer minutes to unnecessary, data-heavy deep dives in order to invest those valuable minutes in more memorable corporate storytelling.

Step 2: Elements of Thickness

Compelling Title

As we explored in Chapter Six, a strong title does so much more than just state what your talk is about. It presents a clear value to the audience long before you get on stage to speak. Your title should combine the challenge and solution into one line that shows you know exactly what problem the attendee needs to solve and precisely how your talk will do it. Rather than "The Future of AI in Auto Manufacturing," try "Why AI Will Be a Benefit to Auto Workers Instead of a Burden." The first title instills fear and sounds stiff; the second instills confidence and sounds compelling, personal, and creative. Rather than "Grant Writing for Cancer Research Laboratories," try "How to Write Grants That Open Doors and Save Lives." The former is solely academic; the latter inspires and sets worthy goals.

Clear Value Proposition

Standard practice is for a speaker to front-load their presentation with challenges and statistics, assuming the audience will eventually see the payoff by the end, once all the details have been laid out. But this is not how humans process spoken messages. Until we know why we should invest our energy and undivided attention, we won't. Never assume your audience will "get it" as your talk progresses; if they don't get it at the start, they'll be long gone by slide five. Spell out each key value for your audience right at the opening of your talk, before you dive into any core content. Ensure they see the immediate benefit to themselves, personally or professionally, so they have a compelling reason to put away their mobile devices and give you their full focus from word one.

The Moment Before

Most speakers make the mistake of leaping straight into content the moment they've finished introducing themselves. Instead, give yourself and your audience a moment to settle in and connect with you on a recognizable human level before delivering any important data or statistics. Until we know and trust you, we aren't fully on your side. Greet us as friends before you treat us like customers. Honor the importance of the occasion, respect your guests' time and attention, and express how excited you are to share your knowledge for our benefit. This moment before will help tamp down pre-talk jitters, foster trust and buy-in, and set your entire talk up for connective success.

Establish the Why

In *Start with Why*, Simon Sinek makes the argument that people don't buy what we do, they buy why we do it.[16] Establish your why before you leap into your what or how. Why do you care so much about this topic, and why should your audience care just as much? Why is now the right time for this particular talk, and why are you the best one to deliver it? Why will their investment in you over the next 10, 30, or 60 minutes pay off? If you don't clearly and confidently spell out all these whys up front, your audience may never figure them out on their own.

Personal Experience

Nothing is more compelling for an audience than a speaker who clearly understands their current needs and gives them the exact value they've

---

16   Sinek (n 4).

been searching for. Before digging into core content, prove that you speak your viewers' language and share their challenges and dreams. When your personal experience looks and sounds familiar, your stories and their stories align. Your attendees get the chance to know and appreciate you before you begin pitching them on your product. Inject your own life experiences into your content to establish familiarity and commonality, turning a dry lecture into a satisfying, human-to-human conversation.

Deeper Meaning

Claims of market superiority and product value are meaningless without context and specific, inspirational applicability for your audience. Generic brags like "Our solution will increase sales," or "We improve your performance by 50%," are nothing more than advertisements, more forgettable salvos in their daily bombardment of attention grabs. This sort of self-aggrandizement hints at desperation, just *low-value* or *no-value* fodder. Work to find the deeper meaning in your message. Instead of "Our solution will increase sales," try "We'll help you respond to your customer faster and keep them happier so they stick around and invest more heavily in your brand." Rather than "We improve your performance by 50%," try "We want to help you spend less time on busywork and more time doing what you love." Deeper meaning plays to personal rather than corporate values, and that's what your audience is looking for. Speak to their hearts instead of their wallets.

Agenda as a Promise

Your agenda is not a grocery list to be ticked off item by item. It's a detailed, multipoint promise to your audience that every part of your talk will be valuable and has been crafted for their success. Each topic you plan to cover is another inspiring opportunity, one more benefit in easy reach. Once they see how many options are on the way and why each will pay off for them, they get excited by your agenda rather than just hoping it all passes by quickly.

Challenge One / Solution One

Standard fare is to lay out every challenge your audience (or the industry) is facing all at once in a lengthy barrage of daily obstacles to success. This faulty presentation strategy overwhelms and irritates rather than inspires and motivates. If you were taught to start with the problem, not the solution, it's time to reassess. Your audience already sees how difficult their work lives are; they don't need you to remind them in a frustrating, negative grocery list. They're thinking, "Stop describing my problems and give me a solution!" If that first solution doesn't arrive quickly, you run the risk of losing or confusing them. Build your challenges and solutions like a game of bowling. You would never bowl all 10 frames at the same time because you'd have to knock down 120 pins with a single ball. Each challenge is one frame only, 10 pins, easily targeted, and easy to eliminate. Start with the biggest, most pressing audience/industry challenge first, then prove how you can successfully remove that one challenge from their lives before moving on to the next.

Immediate Value of Result

You just bowled a strike, expertly defining and solving your audience's biggest shared challenge. They're quickly excited and invested in your talk because you've proven value to them. Before rolling straight into the next frame, the next challenge and solution, stop! Make sure your audience fully internalizes and understands how to easily and instantly apply the better practice you've just dropped into their laps. Don't assume they have automatically connected the dots for themselves; lay it out for them. Tie that single solution back as proof of your opening value proposition. Solidify your first key takeaway in their minds and hearts with a clean, clear example of what they can expect to achieve by taking action as soon as your talk concludes.

Proof of Value

Nothing proves value more than a story that looks and sounds just like our own. Once your audience has experienced the value you just provided in your first challenge/solution, take the time to paint a beautiful picture of how that value will pay off for them. This often occurs through a customer success story or client testimonial. Unfortunately, most customer success stories don't land with an audience because hearing about someone else's success is meaningless until we understand how to achieve that same success ourselves. Your audience won't care about that other company's victory, just about their own. It's your job to give any customer success story enough context to ensure your viewers see themselves as the star of that story, achieving an equally beneficial victory in their own organization.

Challenge Two / Solution Two

Once you've completed the story of your audience's most pressing challenge, you're ready to move on to the next important obstacle to success your audience is experiencing. Time to bowl the next frame. Again, focus only on this second challenge and solution—10 pins and the single value you offer to knock them down.

Immediate Value of Result

As before, don't rush on to your third challenge before solidifying the second solution in their hearts and minds. Stick with challenge/solution two long enough to ensure your audience fully processes and internalizes the next key takeaway you just delivered. Connect it back as another proof of your opening value proposition, and offer a motivating example of the amazing payoff waiting for your viewers thanks to you and your talk.

Proof of Value

Shore up that second deep value by personalizing your solution to this audience. Paint a colorful picture based on another brand's victory, then reframe that success story for this unique set of viewers and their needs. Make sure your attendees recognize the full measure of what product two makes possible for them before you move on to challenge/solution three.

Challenge Three / Solution Three

If your story has a third important challenge and solution to address, give them every bit as much conviction and attention as the first two. But three is the maximum. More than three big ideas in a single talk dilutes the power of your presentation, overwhelming your audience and undermining the memorability of your content. You've heard the expression "always leave them wanting more"—if you have more than three challenges to address, add a second talk. Better yet, save your additional solutions for follow-up conversations after this talk ends. Let attendees know you have a lot more to share and schedule a meeting to discuss their needs. You've bowled three frames together, but the game still has seven frames to go as soon as they're ready. It's a great strategy.

Immediate Value of Result

This is your final opportunity to call back to your original value promise. Everything you have shared with your audience should have pointed directly to that promise, and now you've offered three powerful ways to eliminate the primary obstacles blocking their impending success.

Proof of Value

Find one more story that looks and sounds just like theirs and that shows the compelling difference you and your services make in the lives of others. Your audience has seen what's possible; now you're ready to help them take their first steps toward a brighter future. It's time to head into your conclusion.

Restatement of Key Values

In the sixth grade, you learned an important lesson on essay writing: "Tell them what you're going to tell them; tell them; tell them what you told them." You opened your talk with personal, meaningful value. You delivered that value in multiple ways, with several proof points that brought your story to life in a recognizable, accessible way. Now remind them of all the value paths to success awaiting them, with a confident nod to the fact that you made your viewers a promise and delivered on it. You have earned the right to ask them to make a promise to you in return.

Mark Your Agenda "Complete"

Consider briefly returning to your agenda to show all that you have accomplished within the allotted time frame. This proves to your audience that you can be counted on to deliver on your promises, suggesting you are equally likely to show that same care and passion for them and their customers.

Strong Call to Action

Now that you've delivered on your promise to the audience, you get to ask them for a promise in return—a promise that they'll take an easily achievable first or next step toward new success thanks to you and your presentation. Give your listeners everything they need to walk out of your session with intent and determination to take that leap. Explain exactly what you want them to do next, how long it will take, and when you want them to do it. Light their path so there's no chance they'll get lost or give up before they get started. A strong call to action is your final gift to your audience, sending them out with energy, enthusiasm, and excitement for their own success.

Genuine Conclusion

The last piece of a satisfyingly thick presentation structure is gratitude. A basic thank you and goodbye aren't enough because they discount and discard the audience rather than acknowledging and appreciating them. Take time to demonstrate humility and heartfelt recognition of the gifts of their valuable time and attention. Remind them how much you appreciate their interest, and then open your door to continued conversation. Never say goodbye until you set up the next hello.

These are just some of the numerous elements you can layer, one on top of the other, to create a thick, satisfying, and compelling presentation. Laid out in spreadsheet format, a 30-minute session might look something like this:

SECT.	ELEMENT	TIME (26 minutes)
1	Welcome and Setup	00:00–00:30
2	Value Proposition	00:30–1:30
3	Personal Introduction and Expertise / Your Why	1:30–2:30
4	Agenda	2:30–3:00
5	Challenge One / Solution One	3:00–6:00
6	Demo One	6:00–8:00
7	Proof of Concept / Value Restatement One	8:00–9:00
8	Challenge Two / Solution Two	9:00–13:00
9	Demo Two	13:00–14:30
10	Proof of Concept / Value Restatement Two	14:30–16:00
11	Challenge Three / Solution Three	16:00-19:30
12	Demo Three	19:30-22:30
13	Proof of Concept / Value Restatement Three	22:30–23:30
14	Restatement of Value Proposition	23:30–24:00
15	Call to Action	24:00–25:00
16	Wrap-Up and Sign-Off	25:00–26:00

Figure 7.1 Sample schedule for a thick presentation

Notice that I've only used 26 minutes for a 30-minute scheduled session. This is deliberate, and here's why. With 30 available minutes, a speaker will plan to fill that full allotted time, which leaves no room for variables. For example, what if the prior session runs over by a minute or two and eats into your time? What if attendees need an extra couple of minutes to find your breakout room and make their way to a seat? What if you encounter a technical glitch or get a good question that takes an extra minute to answer? Build in a buffer to allow for flexibility and relaxed delivery.

Even if none of these delays occur, consider the extra few free minutes a gift to your grateful audience. While going over the time limit invites frustration, no one ever got mad at a speaker for giving them bonus time to answer an email, use the bathroom, or grab a cup of coffee before the next talk begins.

We'll use this same graphic again in Chapter Twelve as you draft the script for your upcoming talk. Which elements you choose to include are entirely up to you. Use them all, or use just a few, but the more you offer to your audience, the thicker your talk will be. Develop your own ideas, with these elements serving as a springboard to create more satisfying presentations that help you stand out from the crowd. Each step in the thickness strategy will provide more value, include more passion, and improve connection to your content, helping viewers to retain more of your message over a longer time frame.

DAVID KOVAC

Magician | New Vaudevillian

A school for wizards actually exists. A hidden place where aspiring conjurers study sleight of hand, mind reading, and stage illusions. Here you will also find the next generation of escape artists, jugglers, puzzle enthusiasts, and all manner of ardent mystery mavens. But here's the real secret: They're not learning tricks. They are seeking to become storytellers—magical storytellers.

By night, Hollywood's famed Magic Castle is an elegant private club for adults. By day, Junior Society members gather in the Inner Circle to learn how to cast spells. Like all the greats before them, these youngsters are discovering how to frame their feats of legerdemain, how to engage spectators with enchanting anecdotes, and how to make a memory. One thing you won't hear is "pick a card." Nobody ever cared about a five of clubs. Students must discover how to craft a powerful story.

Just as an audience does not mentally separate the singer from the song, they also do not separate the magician from the trick. Ultimately, there is only the performance. The experience. The thing that connects the magician to the material (and, consequently, the material to the audience) is always the story.

This is why David Copperfield weaves a tale about a child seeing snow for the first time; he does not say, "Here's a stunt with five tons of confetti." Penn & Teller pretend to burn the American flag, not some meaningless swath of blank cloth. David Blaine is known for crafting impossible scenarios that are bizarre, creepy, or intensely dangerous; why stick a long, sharp needle through a party balloon when your own bare arm is, well, closer?

When you combine a strong illusion with a compelling narrative, the quality and impact of the magic increase dramatically. Presto—you've just turned a simple trick into an unforgettable theatrical event! A powerful story has always been the magician's best-kept secret.

CHAPTER EIGHT

START STRONG, END STRONG

THE OPENING IS THE MOST IMPORTANT PART OF ANY STORY. THE truth of this ubiquitous trope is time tested and undeniable, equally applicable across all disciplines and circumstances. When you start strong, you buy considerable goodwill for everything that follows.

In chess, the opening move sets a strategic foundation for the series of attacks and maneuvers on a march to victory. In the news, a headline exists to make you hungry for the report to come. For novelists, the first paragraph sets the tone of the tale, sending readers on a journey of discovery and revelation. As a speaker, the way you open your talk can make or break your session. It could instantly connect you and your message to your audience, or it could instantly build an insurmountable barrier that's impossible to overcome.

The conclusion of your story is equally vital; it's your chance to leave a lasting impact on your viewers or to leave them high and dry. A movie that starts strong but ends weak sends us out the door feeling frustrated and disappointed. A restaurant that opens with a brilliant appetizer but concludes with a mediocre dessert is less likely to earn a return visit. A talk that opens with a bang but ends with a whimper is incomplete and quickly forgotten. There is no point in showing time and care for the opening pitch and then neglecting to deliver in the final chapter. You say goodbye and your audience thinks, "Wait … that's it?"

Think of the beginning and end of your presentation as crucial book-ends, framing your story with value and purpose from the first word to the last. One pulls your audience into your world, while the other gives them wings to fly the moment you set them free. Without both of these bookends, the center has no structure and collapses. Let's start with your opening bookend.

An Introduction They Can Invest In

At the start of an average talk, the speaker will introduce themselves and the title of their topic, give a brief, business-card-style job description, then race instantly into core content. Pay attention the next time you're watching a presentation, and notice how rapidly the speaker transitions from "Hello" to their first content slide. It'll give you whiplash. The faster they stop talking about themselves and dive into corporate speak, the less thought they've given to their viewers and the less satisfying their talk will be, guaranteed. You've seen this happen countless times but probably never knew the telltale signs; now you do.

As we discussed in the previous chapter, when your audience is given no opportunity to connect with you as the speaker before being hit with the hard sell, your job becomes much more difficult. Remember, the opening of your talk is about them, not you or your brand. They've already read your name, session title, and bio and decided to attend, so open with a story instead of a sales pitch.

Your front bookend establishes value and demonstrates passion your viewers, creating connection, trust, and credibility. This setup can't be skipped or minimized in a desperate rush toward product detail and data; with no foundation, your audience is left in the dust. You can't simply cut and paste preexisting content into a strong opening; you have to demonstrate passion and personal perspectives on your topic in a way that makes you likable and recognizable to your attendees.

I'll reiterate that your audience won't invest in you or your message until they clearly see the value for themselves in your talk, either personally, professionally, or both. Commit real, dedicated time in the opening of your talk to focus on your listeners and their needs before introducing your own content messaging. This strategy alone will set you apart from the majority of speakers.

How much time this thick, layered, and highly orchestrated opening will take depends on you and how much of yourself you're willing to give. Let's compare a typical 20–30 second opening with no personal investment to one that takes a bit longer but offers so much more to the listener:

> Hi, I'm Steve. I'm a futurist and technical data engineer with XYZ Corporation, and today I want to talk about establishing a baseline for successful DevOps evolution. We're going to look at the most recent DevOps report, which is the world's largest body of DevOps knowledge, then we'll see three different technologies XYZ has built to address the changes in our new, hybrid marketplace. I'll show you how they work then give you some customer examples of best practices. Let's get started.

This is actually longer than most speakers take to make their introduction. But it's still too thin and self-serving. I blast through my opening talking about myself and my company, never putting the focus on my audience. I offer nothing connective or personal, I reveal no passion for either my topic or my attendee's success, and I make no promises that excite my listeners to lean in and gift me their attention. It's straight to business, and because I haven't established rapport, trust, or credibility, my audience is less inclined to invest in my story. All I can do is hope they'll eventually recognize my value.

By racing to the data, I have put myself in a weakened and compromised position as a speaker. I've saved myself some effort and maximized time for core technical content but sacrificed the likelihood my audience will care about any of it. With no enticing picture in their heads of how my proposed solutions will lead to their personal success, they're unlikely to give full focus to me or my talk. This introduction is perfunctory, no fun to deliver, and neglectful of my viewers.

Now I'll invest more time and effort in the opening of my presentation, adding value, passion, and connection for the benefit of my respected audience members:

Good morning! What an exciting and rewarding time we get to work in these days. Whether you are a developer or an engineer or a systems manager or the IT lead for your organization, you are the ones out there every day creating the new code as infrastructure. You build the automation. You invent the culture that defines the tools of today and tomorrow. And I'm so inspired by the great work that you do and that we do together. My name is Steve, and as one of you, I keep asking myself, "Can we be doing even better? Can we get faster, cheaper, even more reliable?" The answer is yes, absolutely, and in the next thirty minutes you'll see how. Sound good?

I'm a DevOps strategy guy and a tech explorer by nature. I lead global cross-functional teams in marketing, sales, and partnership skills. I've even won a few awards for it! Today I get to put all my experience to work for all of you. We'll look at ways to develop your own next-level service operations. We'll check out new implementation methods so you're totally up to speed. I'll even show you a couple of my favorite DevOps tools so you can add them to your own tool belts.

On my way in today, I was talking with a college buddy who just left her job and decided to hang out her own consulting shingle. She asked me, "Steve, how do I get this solo ball rolling?" and I told her there is no right or wrong way; you just do what feels right and works best for you. Because building something new is nonlinear. Same with DevOps—it's nonlinear. There's no one "right way" to explore. But there are three key avenues to get you where you want to go: standardization, reduced variability, and self-service. And today, I'm going to get you moving on all three. Let's do this!

That introduction took four times longer to deliver than the first iteration, but look at the massive difference an additional 90-second investment creates. These two openings to the same talk place my audience in entirely different states of receptiveness, attention, and anticipation.

This second introduction delivers energy, passion, intent, and value for my viewers. By the time I get to my core technical content, my audience is completely on board and invested in me and my message. They can hear how excited I am, recognize my interest in helping them succeed, and see me as one of them. All these initial positive responses at the top of my talk will pay off again and again as my presentation unfolds, ensuring deeper engagement and commitment and "stickier" content. Well worth an extra minute and a half.

My longer intro means I now have to remove those additional 90 seconds from somewhere else in my content. This is fine, since my audience is only likely to retain 3%–8% of everything I share in the next 25 minutes. I'm glad to cut 90 seconds of statistical or product data and allot that time to a more valuable, personal, and connective opening. A couple fewer statistical bullet points won't matter, but investment in immediate connection with my guests at the start of my talk will pay impressive dividends.

A Conclusion That Inspires Action

The conclusion of your talk is every bit as important as the opening. Too often, a speaker reaches their last slide, asks the audience to reach out to their sales rep, says thank you, and just walks away. It's a losing strategy.

By the end of a strong presentation, the speaker has hopefully earned the trust and respect of their listeners, and now it's time to seal the deal. Your closing bookend deserves as much strategy and planning as your opening statement. A strong ending requires a strong directive, one that points the audience to a better destination ahead, even if you won't be around to see them reach that destination.

When a novelist concludes their book, the end is usually just that—the end. Perhaps the stage is set for a sequel, but it begs nothing more of the reader than to stand by and wait for the next installment to be published. When a chess player mates their opponent, the game is over; there is no next step other than to reset the board for a new match. The end of your talk demands much more because it is not, in fact, the end. It is only the beginning. The end of a good presentation is an open door and invitation to a next step, toward a better and more successful future. Deliver your closing words correctly, and your message will last long after you've left the spotlight.

Public presentations die when they abruptly fizzle out with nothing more than a simple thank you. All those promises made by the title and abstract, generous welcome setup, deep-dive content, and promised value lead nowhere. The audience is simply dismissed, left to wonder what they should do with everything they've just heard and seen. Your last gift to your viewers must be a clear and easy instruction on what happens next and how to achieve the success you've just finished explaining or demonstrating.

If you dedicated an extra 90 seconds to your personal introduction, how much time should you dedicate to a strong conclusion? The answer is as long as it takes to be just as passionate, connective, and inspiring as you were at the start of your talk. Don't rush. It isn't enough to just toss up a URL and expect the audience to download your software and learn how to use it. The percentage who will actually visit that URL is extremely low and the number who will take the time and effort to download and learn your software on their own is even lower.

Bookend your talk with a reminder of your original value proposition and how you promised to get them moving toward this beautiful new vision easily, quickly, and with minimal investment. Detail the ways you will remain available to help them get where you suggest they go. Express your desire to extend this new speaker-audience relationship you've just established. Never say goodbye until you've set up the next hello.

Here is a weak call to action that is likely to net poor results, if any at all:

> So, that's all the slides I have. If you want to learn more, go to our microsite and download the reports. Or you can reach out to your sales rep for a test drive. Thank you.

Here is how I would convert that uninspiring, lazy call to action into a strong and motivating directive. This will take me 90 seconds longer to deliver, but it will be so much more valuable and inspirational for my attendees and increase the likelihood of proactive follow-through:

> As I said at the start of our session, we live in the most exciting and rewarding times. You are the developers, engineers, and IT experts creating the new code as infrastructure, building the automation, and inventing the culture. And you've just seen three ways we can do it even better, faster, cheaper, and more reliably. Let's make that happen together. Grab your mobile phone right now and open up your calendar. I want you to create a new appointment with me for next week on whatever day works best for you. Just a quick, five-minute call, nothing more. There's my number on the screen. Got it? Great. Send me that request, and I'll get you moving forward right away.
>
> Between now and next week when we talk, here is that "first steps" methodology chart I promised to share with you. I've also

got hard copies if you want to put one in your bag. Introduce yourself or shoot me an email and I'll send you a link to share with your team. If you want to try that new interface I showed you, excellent! Let me buy you a coffee and we can walk through the dashboard together. Then, if you see me at tonight's customer appreciation event, beers are on me!

Again, I'm Steve, and my team and I are here to help. We'll be right there with you every step of the way to make amazing things happen for your team. I can't wait to hear your success stories!

This call to action is going to net a high response rate. It's fun, friendly, encouraging, and offers multiple easy actions to follow up on. I continue to deliver value, passion, and connection right up to the last word of my talk, and my audience walks away feeling inspired and motivated. I've tied a direct through line from the opening bookend of my presentation to the closing bookend, leaving viewers with a warm offer of continued partnership. They get one last reminder of the benefits I promised from the start, and I've shown them exactly how to put those new benefits to work right away while my content is still fresh in their minds. I've even set up our next meeting and offered multiple paths to extend our business relationship. All with a small investment of an additional one and a half minutes.

What do you think your viewers will remember more: a strong conclusion like this or a few more KPIs?

When You Say "Thank You," Mean "Thank You"

Your gratitude should be genuine and heartfelt, a worthy acknowledgment of the substantial gifts of time and focus your audience has just given to you. The words "thank you" tossed out at the end as an afterthought are not enough; your guests deserve better. Script your thanks as you script any other piece of your story—with personal passion that sends attendees off feeling heard, valued, and proud of themselves for choosing to spend their valuable time in your session. A successful thank you sounds something like this:

> I've really enjoyed our last thirty minutes together. I know it's a busy conference day, and you've already got so much to think about. I hope you gained a lot of new value from my talk and that you're excited to make these ideas your own. If there's any way I can support you, please reach out. Mostly, I want to thank you for your time, your interest, and for allowing me to share my story today. I'd love to hear your story next. Go make great things happen!

There is nothing corporate in this conclusion, just a connective, audience-focused appreciation for the time you've shared. Leave your audience with this last moment of positivity, and your talk will stick around longer in their hearts and minds.

— SEAN GRENNAN —

Playwright | Actor

It's hard to imagine a world without storytelling. There certainly wouldn't be much on Netflix. Sure, we'd have sports, but even those events tell stories: We assign bravery, cunning, and virtue to the winners and cowardice, dullness, and vice to the losers. Even if the team just ... lost. From the time we're read to as children, stories help us figure out what it is to be human, to have friends, to love, to hate, to stumble, and to simply survive.

There's always been a tension in people's minds between which is more important, the "science" umbrella, covering things like math, engineering, or chemistry, or the "storytelling" umbrella, covering theatre, movies, literature, or design. In *Shakespeare: The Invention of the Human*, noted critic and author Harold Bloom posits that those watching Shakespeare's plays glean life lessons, new language, and expanded ways of thinking, loving, and understanding human nature, in others and in ourselves.[17]

It's been said that "writers are explaining the world to themselves." We're all natural storytellers, striving to understand our reality. We pass someone on the street wearing expensive jewelry and instantly start to write the story of how they got their money. They're a drug dealer or a stockbroker. Or they inherited that wealth and never worked a day in their life. We see a story, and we make up new stories of our own.

As a playwright, I create stories to understand why we do what we do, why we make the same mistakes, why we reach higher, and what it means when we succeed or fail. My first goal is to draw the audience in, and my greatest success is when that audience sees themselves onstage. "Hey, my mom is like that," or "Wow, that is exactly how I would feel!" Ideally, that audience takes something away that tweaks their thinking about themselves and the world. Sometimes they simply escape for two hours. There is no one-size-fits-all story, no definition of a winner or loser. The sciences, engineering, and medicine all make life possible; storytelling tells us why. And telling the story is what makes life worth living.

---

17   Bloom, Harold. *Shakespeare: The Invention of the Human*. New York: Riverhead Books, 1999.

CHAPTER NINE

PROVE VALUE FIRST / PROVE VALUE ALWAYS

As I've repeatedly stated, until your audience clearly recognizes, understands, and internalizes the value of your talk for them, they won't gift you with their full attention or invest in the details you plan to share. The moment you step into the spotlight, before you say a word about your brand or product, you have to prove value for your viewers. *Prove value first (PVF)*.

Once your audience internalizes that value and leans in to hear how to achieve it, you have to repeat that value again and again throughout your talk. You must continually connect each new piece of data to your original value proposition, reminding them throughout your talk about what got them excited to begin with. After every section or solution, point out how each element represents meaningful improvement in their status quo. *Prove value always (PVA)*.

My acronym could just as easily be PVF, PVAAAA: Prove value first, prove value again and again and again … and again. You get the idea.

Prove Value First

Dr. Martin Luther King Jr. said, "Faith is taking the first step even when you don't see the whole staircase." The first words of your talk provide a special opportunity for your audience to establish faith in you and in your message to come. Without the full picture in their minds, your promise of forthcoming value is the hook that will grab their attention. And grab it you must, immediately and confidently. As we explored in the last chapter, a strong beginning establishes the why of your talk, both for you and your listeners, setting the tone for your entire session.

Prove value first is about launching your presentation with a story instead of with your title, résumé, agenda, or product. Since nothing gets sold until the story gets told, your *prove value first* strategy gets your story and its goals for success off to a powerful start. You'll eliminate any risk that your attendees might be hesitant or skeptical and instantly assure them they've already won just by choosing to attend your talk.

Prove value first demonstrates to your listener that you have their best interests at heart, even before your own. They hear their biggest challenges addressed right up front, along with a promise to solve those challenges during your short time together. Hearing this value at the start guides your audience to anticipate the benefits you are about to provide. *Prove value first* sounds like this:

> Thank you all for joining me today. I'm so excited about our time together because, in the next twenty minutes, I get to help you gain [BENEFIT A], [BENEFIT B], and [BENEFIT C]. By the time we're done, you'll quickly and easily be ready to achieve [VALUE ONE] faster than ever before. You'll deliver [VALUE TWO] with more confidence and strength. And you'll finally realize [VALUE THREE] in a way that sets you apart from your competition and gets your organization right where you want to be. My name is [XXX] and I'm a [JOB TITLE] with [BRAND X] ...

Thirty seconds into this talk, and the audience knows exactly what to expect. They hear passion in the speaker, a dedication to their success, and solid focus on their goals. They know precisely what the speaker plans to do for them. They are instantly confident this talk is worth their time and attention. It's clear the speaker has put them first instead of prioritizing themselves or their own brand. And they have yet to hear a résumé, see an agenda, or read a single key performance indicator. And, because so few talks begin this way, *prove value first* creates differentiation for this speaker and session.

Countless books have been written on how to open a talk with strength and magnetism. Blogs and self-proclaimed best practice guides offer generic suggestions like "Open with a joke," or "Tell a funny story," or "Shock or surprise your audience to gain their interest." These methods rarely work as they take a speaker off topic, waste time, and force inorganic behavior that creates discomfort in delivery.

As a presenter, you may worry about how to create value without statistical data to rely on, or that the value you intend to offer isn't the value your attendees want to hear. What if the audience won't pay attention, misses a key piece of information, or doesn't find your content compelling? What if they pay more attention to their mobile phones than to your talk? *Prove value first* puts these concerns to rest, instilling confidence in both your audience and in you as the speaker.

Prove value first by focusing on what you know best and are already passionate about:

> My team and I have spent the last two years focused on a groundbreaking wastewater management solution that I finally have the chance to share with all of you today. In the next forty-five minutes, we're going to change how we build our communities, how we design our local infrastructures, and what we pass along to our children. I'm so looking forward to what our companies will do together in the next six months.

Your audience doesn't need the joke, the laugh, or the shock; they just need to get immediately invested and recognize how much you have to offer them. There's nothing wrong with a good joke, but it's not required.

Value earns attention organically, without the pressure to solicit laughs. A wise adage, often credited to Theodore Roosevelt, says that "people don't care how much you know until they know how much you care." *Prove value first* is the best way to show you care, through clear, undeniable benefit from the moment you open your mouth.

The Value of Stand-Up MRI

I represented a powerful radiology manufacturer who had developed an impressive new method for scanning patients in load-bearing positions. It made perfect sense; if your knee hurts, you should be scanned standing on that knee instead of lying down. However, their technology faced skepticism from the deeply conservative radiology establishment and resistance from the insurance industry, which didn't want to pay for more costly, "niche" procedures deemed elective instead of essential. Hoping to win over the crowd, this manufacturer took numerous marketing missteps in their outbound messaging.

My client's initial strategy was to open each talk with a storied retrospective of their brand, including a boastful history of how the system had been developed and the numerous awards and accolades they'd won. They were tooting their own horn so loudly that they couldn't hear their attendees' apathy. The technology was impressive, but the corporate story lacked passion or connection. It was a desperate and obvious plea for buyers, and assumed a "wow" factor alone would inspire attendees to instantly leap on board. It didn't. The audience couldn't have cared less. We had to change the message and create the connection. We had to *prove value first*.

Step one was to scrap the ego and kick off each talk with daily patient realities, stories from the very clinics and hospitals our attendees owned and operated. We shifted to the exact words of customers, telling us how difficult it was to properly diagnose patient symptoms and how much harder their jobs were when patients couldn't be assessed in the exact stress positions that created their painful symptoms. We shared financial concerns, space limitations, and the potential for better results and profits. By the first mention of our brand, three minutes into the talk, we had proven value and developed a stronger, more meaningful connection with our audience. And we still hadn't even said the name of our new product.

Our technology didn't matter until the audience was prioritized first, personally acknowledged, appreciated, and respected. Before investing in our message, those radiologists had to recognize that our primary focus was on them instead of on the desires of our brand or our pride in the awards we'd received. *Prove value first* helped us reach more people more quickly, leading to a more positive response.

Saving the big payoff for the end of your talk is a public speaking no-no. This "big reveal" storytelling approach works in spy movies and novels but not in presentations. Viewers won't follow you through an entire 30-minute session just hoping to recognize the value by the time you've wrapped up. They have to know why it's worth sticking around. When you delay your value until after you've laid out all the evidence, you risk losing them long before you get there. And, once you've lost them, they're probably not coming back. Nobody decides halfway through a conversation, "Oh, I think I'll start paying attention now."

Establishing value at the start of your talk is the first half of a winning presentation equation. The second half is keeping your audience engaged and connected to you and your content until the call to action.

Prove Value Always

You've proven value first, and now you have to follow up on that opening value promise through every phase of your talk. We've all seen films that fail to deliver on a fantastic trailer; the carefully crafted teaser draws us in with anticipation for a great story to come. Then it soon becomes clear that those moments selected for the trailer are the only moments of the movie worth watching. A promising first look has to continue paying off over and over throughout the story to keep your audience invested.

Prove value always means repeatedly and consistently returning to and restating your opening value proposition across each part of your presentation, re-hooking your viewers again and again as you go. PVF only happens once, but PVA happens numerous times—a strategy that takes a bit longer to explain and craft.

Once into the meat of your talk, you want to keep reminding your listeners of the powerful payoffs that first got them excited about—and invested in—your topic. Not because those listeners are bored or tired or ignorant, but because each new piece of information you share, each data point, technical breakdown, and key performance indicator, requires bandwidth and memory to process. The more you add, the more your viewers are asked to absorb and the further you separate your audience from your original *prove value first* proposition.

In a long talk (or a long day filled with talks), an attendee becomes mired in statistical overload, forgetting the big picture value of "What's in it for me?" *Prove value always* repeatedly calls back to your opening promise, connecting the dots for your audience and ensuring they never forget why choosing your session was such a smart decision.

Of course, this repetition adds time to your presentation, time that must be reallocated from other, more dense sections of your talk. Do it. Just like your strong opening and closing statements, that redistribution away from statistical facts and figures is a wise tradeoff.

Many speakers mistakenly assume that one mention of any piece of information is enough, that there is no need to repeat content, and that redundancy may even seem disrespectful to an audience. Psychology disagrees. Redundancy is proven to be vital to comprehension, and you should use it deliberately and liberally to solidify your value in the listener's mind.

A 2015 study by professors Susanne Schmidt and Martin Eisend measured repeated marketing message impact and the minimum requirement for reliable consumer response. In their results, titled *Advertising Repetition: A Meta-Analysis on Effective Frequency in Advertising*,[18] Schmidt and Eisend determined that maximum response to information is reached at approximately

---

18   Schmidt, Susanne, and Martin Eisend. "Advertising Repetition: A Meta-Analysis on Effective Frequency in Advertising." *Journal of Advertising* 44, no. 4 (2015): 415–428. https://doi.org/10.1080/00913367.2015.1018460.

10 exposures. While recall increases linearly, it does not begin to level off before the eighth exposure. In other words, your viewers may not fully internalize or even recognize the value you're offering in your talk until that value has been restated at least eight times, possibly 10, and maybe more.

Ten times? Any speaker who repeats the exact same message 10 times will quickly face a hostile audience. Repeated messaging requires nuance, variety, and creativity. *Prove value always* encourages repetition for maximum exposure, but through varied angles that offer multiple perspectives on the same big picture payoffs.

In 1885, London's Thomas Smith Agency published one of the earliest advocate studies of effective frequency called *Successful Advertising: Its Secrets Explained.* This handbook by Smith and J. H. Osborne proposed an intriguing formula that remains revelatory to this day:

The 1st time people look at an ad, they don't see it.

The 2nd time, they don't notice it.

The 3rd time, they are aware that it is there.

The 4th time, they have a fleeting sense that they've seen it before.

The 5th time, they actually read the ad.

The 6th time, they thumb their nose at it.

The 7th time, they get a little irritated with it.

The 8th time, they think, "Here's that confounded ad again."

The 9th time, they wonder if they're missing out on something.

The 10th time, they ask their friends or neighbors if they've tried it.

The 11th time, they wonder how the company is paying for all these ads.

The 12th time, they start to think that it must be a good product.

The 13th time, they start to feel the product has value.

The 14th time, they start to feel like they've wanted a product like this for a long time.

The 15th time, they start to yearn for it because they can't afford to buy it.

The 16th time, they accept the fact that they will buy it sometime in the future.

The 17th time, they make a commitment to buy the product.

The 18th time, they curse their poverty because they can't buy this terrific product.

The 19th time, they count their money very carefully.

The 20th time prospects see the ad, they buy what it is offering.[19]

Smith and Osborne's bedrock formula boils down to *frequency = understanding*. And while they were speaking about advertising rather than public presentations, their rule of repetition can be applied equally, with slight variation.

In advertising, a brand makes inroads using slogans such as "Just do it," "Got milk?" "I'm lovin' it," and "Fifteen minutes could save you 15% or more on car insurance." Repetition of these brand bylines eventually seeps into the marketplace psyche and molds public perception, positive or negative, of a brand or product. Repetition builds connection, and over time, that connection (hopefully) creates successful business bonds. "Like a good neighbor, State Farm is there" has been an endless echo since 1971. DeBeers has been telling us "A diamond is forever" since 1947. "Good to the last drop" has been repeated millions of times by Maxwell House since 1915.

Of course, slogans aren't value statements, and when we give a public presentation, it's the value that matters, not the brand. When we *prove value first* in a talk, we are launching with a specific and personal promise of success that addresses current challenges to professional or personal growth. Maxims alone are not enough. The repetition required to achieve Smith and Osborne's *frequency = understanding* formula relies on a series of varied callbacks to the overarching value proposition. Luckily, speakers have far more time and opportunity to build a repeatable value case for an audience than the 5–60 seconds most advertisers are afforded.

To demonstrate how *prove value always* is easier to implement than you may think, say the title of your talk is "Better Curriculum Design for Greater Student Success." Opening your presentation, you *prove value first* by

---

19   Smith, Thomas, and J. H. Osborne. *Successful Advertising: Its Secrets Explained.* London: Smith's Advertising Agency, 1885.

promising that, in 30 minutes, the members of your audience will learn to

- Cut course-design time in half.
- Double levels of student engagement from the first exercise to the final test.
- Help classes achieve improved study and higher content-retention rates.
- Increase average scores and long-term student-success results.
- Reduce attrition rates and minimize dropouts.
- Re-energize purpose-driven excitement as an educator.

This already sounds like an excellent presentation, clearly addressing challenges that higher learning professors face every day. Your content agenda is complex and detailed, including recent curriculum structure methods, fresh approaches to course design, and advanced technologies supporting educators in their professional journeys. Your audience is prepared and ready to learn these new success strategies, and you are primed to launch into an inspiring, actionable corporate story.

The depth of information in your talk is considerable. Because you hope to accomplish so much, you could run the risk of overwhelming your listeners. You will diminish that risk and keep your audience engaged and re-energized by taking breaks between each element to continually refer them back to your opening *prove value first* statement. Those breaks, where one part of your story ends and the next begins, are where you *prove value always*.

Let's say that Challenge One / Solution One focuses on your recently released software platform that helps a professor build complex interactive videos, virtual reality projects, and software simulations. You spend four minutes describing your platform and walking viewers through the interface. When that part of your talk ends, and before you move on to Challenge Two / Solution Two, stop. Give your audience a moment to fully absorb, process, and internalize the benefit you've just shared, and to imagine using it in their own classrooms.

This is the first of multiple *prove value always* opportunities. Connect your new software back to one or more of your opening promises. Ensure the audience translates what that capability will mean for them the minute they deploy it in their organization. Remind them of the big why. Then you can move on to another compelling concept.

Try a different *prove value always* approach following the next segment in your corporate story: "Remember how I said you'd cut your course-design time in half? What I just demonstrated is proof of how you can make that happen." Then try a different callback: "At the start of my talk, I promised you could improve long-term results for your students. What I just showed you is the first step toward giving them that path to a brighter, more successful future."

As your talk unfolds, moving from point to point and challenge to solution, continue to *prove value always* in slightly varied but repeated reminders of how much your audience is learning and benefiting from your session. After a customer example, make that example accessible to anyone in the room. Demonstrate a graph, then connect it to the big picture success they've been searching for. Tell your audience exactly why every number and quote are meaningful for them. Find a mix of ways to reiterate value to your viewers, helping them to construct an airtight vision of their own success through your corporate story.

Prove value first ignites your audience so they become connected and give you their full and undivided attention. *Prove value always* guarantees that connection and attention never wane. Remember PVF and PVA, and apply these valuable tools to every public talk you deliver.

── DONALD GOOR ──

Rabbi Emeritus of Temple Judea, Tarzana, California
Campus Rabbi at Hebrew Union College–Jewish Institute of
Religion, Jerusalem

Abraham and Sarah were sitting in their tent in the middle of the desert when three strangers wandered by. They immediately welcomed the strangers in, serving them food and drink.

Before God destroyed the world with a mighty flood, Noah, known as a righteous person, walked with God. Following his test of faith, a rainbow appeared to Noah promising that the world would never be destroyed by flood again.

A prince, in ill health, lived a far distance from his parents, the king and queen. He missed them terribly but was afraid he did not have the strength to journey home. When his parents heard, they told him to venture as far as he could and that they would go toward him, meeting him along the way.

These stories teach us moral lessons. Abraham and Sarah model hospitality to strangers. Like Noah, we must act righteously so that we, too, might walk with God. The rainbow challenges us to never allow our world to devolve into evil. The prince and his parents encourage us to meet others halfway. Real or imagined, a great story can inspire our abilities and help us build lives of meaning and purpose.

At the core, a rabbi is a storyteller. We share the narrative of Jewish tradition from the days of the Bible through modern times. Our weekly sermons strive to engage, illuminate, and challenge our congregations through both oral tradition and shared experiences. By telling these stories, we hope to model what is possible. And we hope that our listeners will hear and internalize the lessons we offer, adapting their gifts into more rewarding personal and spiritual journeys.

CHAPTER TEN

ADDING THE PASSION

As I was conducting research for this book, I spent a few days in Las Vegas hosting an event for a group of robotics systems manufacturers. Driving back to my hotel one evening, I heard an interview with Melissa Manchester, the Grammy winner with a long list of power pop hits in the 1970s and 80s. She had taken a lyric writing class with the legendary Paul Simon, who offered what Manchester described as the single most important storytelling lesson of her career; he said, "All the stories have already been told. It's the way you tell your story that's your mark of authenticity."[20]

I heard that quote and thought, "That's it!" Passion is not simply about excitement or enthusiasm or emotional response, it is about the joy of individual authenticity. The way *you* tell *your* story. Whatever talk you are preparing for, the content of your story does not have to be original, special, or earth shattering in order to succeed; it only has to be delivered with passion and rooted in the belief that what you have to share contains meaningful value for others. This was a profound revelation for me, the lesson I'd learned from Grandmother and Aunt Stephanie some 30 years earlier but couldn't quite understand at the time.

Just as legendary songwriters like Melissa Manchester and Paul Simon are not expected to reinvent the word "love" or to prove that their rhymes are better than another writer's rhymes, your audience does not expect you or your corporate story to be one of a kind in order to recognize and

---

20   Manchester, Melissa. Interview By Seth Rudetsky. *Seth Speaks on Broadway*. April 2017.   https://www.melissamanchester.com/did-you-miss-melissas-interview-with-seth -rudetsky-catch-it-here/.

connect with your passion for telling it. As in politics, all stories are local. Passion is equally local. It is experienced by one brave individual—you—willing to get up in front of others and share what matters most to you and why. When we connect our personal passions to the content in our talks, our mark of authenticity shines through.

Public speaking is a gift precisely because it is your opportunity to share your passion for what you care about. When an audience recognizes passion in your communication with them, they become more engaged, invest more deeply, and hope to feel some of that passion for themselves. They are attending your talk to learn and grow with you, and your passion will go a long way toward helping them discover a newfound passion of their own.

So, how and where do you start to add passion to your next talk? It doesn't happen all at once. This is a slow and steady exercise: one point of passion here, another there. Your easiest cue points for inserting why you care so much about your topic are moments of key information delivery, statistics, and transitions.

Moments of Key Information Delivery: Make the Link

Look for any moment in your script where you offer your audience an important nugget of new information such as a recent study, a version update, or a positive change from their longtime status quo. Rather than drop the information and move on, take a moment to follow it up with your personal perspective on why that information is particularly exciting—how it inspires you, terrifies you, or represents something magical for your industry. For example:

> By 2026, global renewable electricity capacity is forecast to rise more than 60% to over 4,800 GW, equivalent to the current total global power capacity of fossil fuels and nuclear combined. Renewables are on track to account for almost 95% of the

increase in global power capacity through 2026.[21] That's 60% in the next five years—think about what that means for your kids, your grandkids, the beach where you take your vacation, and the mountain where your family goes hiking. A 95% increase in renewables is money in your pocket and food on your table and cleaner air and water. That's why I get up every morning and what I go to bed thinking about every night. How can we make it better? The only way we do that is together.

Move through your script to the next moment of new information and repeat the process. What is it about that next metric that makes you feel passionate, that you care deeply about and want to share with your audience? Then move to the next moment and the next. Eventually, you will be speaking with passion throughout your talk, connecting every concept, number, and benefit to your audience with a positive, real-world perspective that brings it all to life.

Statistics Come Alive Through Stories

Data on its own is just a disconnected laundry list of facts and figures. We have little chance of recalling these details once they leave the screen or the speaker's mouth. Make your statistics stickier by adding why they matter, what story they tell, and why your audience needs to commit them to memory. For example:

Crumbling highway infrastructure costs each resident in our state an average of $845 per year, the highest cost in the nation.

21 IEA. "Renewable electricity growth is accelerating faster than ever worldwide, supporting the emergence of the new global energy economy." December 1, 2021. https://www.iea.org/news/renewable-electricity-growth-is-accelerating-faster-than-ever-worldwide-supporting-the-emergence-of-the-new-global-energy-economy.

The average resident in the United States only pays $318 per year. So you are personally shelling out an additional $527 every year for our 148 bridges and more than 860 highway miles labeled "poor" condition by the federal government.[22] Two drivers in your home? That's an extra $1,054 per year. And we're still not getting any of those bridges or highways fixed. Do your kids drive too? Now it's over $2,000 extra out of your family's pocket. We both know what we have to do. Are you as angry about these numbers and how little we're getting for them as I am?

I share the data, and then I share why that data makes me passionate and invested. This powerful one-two punch will lock that information into my viewers' minds, connecting it to an emotional response I would never achieve with statistics alone.

Passion for your topic—and your willingness to share that passion with others—creates a far more successful and longer-lasting impact on your listener than product metrics and technical data ever can or will. A number without a good reason to get excited about that number is a lost opportunity. But when you connect that number to a passionate story, explaining why it matters on a personal, human level, it becomes tangible and real. Metrics and data leap to life when supported by passionate stories that shift the picture from corporate speak to a common vision.

Passion Supports Great Transitions

Every time your story transitions from one idea to the next, from one point of focus to another, that's a perfect spot to add a moment of personal

---

22   U.S. Department of Transportation. "The Bipartisan Infrastructure Law Will Deliver for Rhode Island." Last updated April 11, 2022. https://www.transportation.gov/briefing-room/bipartisan-infrastructure-law-will-deliver-rhode-island.

insight and passionate commentary on what you've just finished describing. For example:

> I just showed you how to calculate the average cost of your company's cloud migration. Before we see the first steps on how to tackle that move successfully, think about why this is so important for us to do as quickly as we possibly can. I love that I only pay for what I actually use. I'm not paying for more resources than my organization needs, and that makes me look like a total rock star. My IT team loves how I've made their jobs so much easier; they spend weekends with their families now, and I love that I've helped play a small part in making that happen. Our migration cut security incidents, and our customers are noticing and smiling. This really excites me, and I hope it excites you too. Here's how to make it happen for your team ...

And you're on to the next section of your talk.

Dig Deep

In theory, passion in your presentations should be easy. If you believe in what you do—in your job, your company, and your product—then you should *want* to share those beliefs with others to help them realize the same benefits you yourself have realized. In reality, finding things to be passionate about in your talk can be intimidating because it means getting personal, adding yourself into your content rather than simply relying on your product's merits alone to get the message across.

Revealing ourselves is risky, and anything too personal is viewed as unnecessary, a waste of time, and a distraction from your measurable core content data. Nothing could be further from the truth. Your audience connects with passion, not data points.

As we've seen, until your audience recognizes your why, they have little interest in the what or how of your product, service, or solution. Why demands passion, and many of us are not very passionate about our jobs or the brands we represent. This is the reason so many glossophobic speakers struggle with how to include passion in their public talks. Discovering your personal passion for why you do what you do means digging deep. Find your story, and you find your passion.

Imagine your company makes disposable rubber gloves. You have been asked to give a talk on the superiority of your brand's gloves at a medical products sales conference and have to create meaningful value for your audience. You don't really have a passion for rubber gloves; they're just your job. So, how will you add passion for this topic into your talk?

Finding passion requires looking beyond the product. Instead of pitching the superiority of your gloves, consider the meaningful benefits your gloves create for others. Think of the indispensable daily role a reliable, safe pair of rubber gloves will play in a chemist's chances of discovering a new vaccine. Or protecting millions of factory workers around the globe from injury. Or allowing the school nurse to safely care for all the children in your community, including your own. Imagine the potential danger an inferior latex glove poses to the medic treating a car-crash victim in your neighborhood parking lot. Or how reliable rubber gloves helped your friend hold her immunocompromised baby's hand in the newborn intensive care unit. Passion isn't about rubber gloves; it's about how your gloves are helping people every day in ways that directly affect your life and the lives of those you'll be giving your presentation to.

I recently supported a Fortune tech brand on a series of international talks for their new software security product. This valuable application lets users expose hidden network threats up to 100 times faster, then remediate those threats in seconds rather than hours. We started our process with the most direct and obvious story, as most marketing typically does:

> Our product helps IT to recognize data breaches at 10× speed, then fix those problems more easily and with less downtime.

Great product but no passion. The initial message was too on the nose and overly corporate with no human perspective. We knew what our product was built to do; now we needed to know why it mattered to our potential customers on a personal level. Where was the passion we hoped to awaken in our audience? That required digging deep and discovering the bigger story, including what led to this particular software development.

I asked my client why they had such faith in their new release and why the industry should care as much as we did. At first, their answers were internally focused and uncreative: "Every company needs to protect themselves from threats. Every IT group wants to find leaks and fix them faster." Agreed. But could we focus on one individual IT user instead of on an entire company or industry? What would our software solution mean to one unique person's day-to-day work life?

"As we said, if an IT guy can discover problems faster, he can fix them more easily."

I wanted to know who this IT guy was, what he was thinking, how the operational change we were offering could improve how he did his job, and how it could reduce the time and energy it took for him to succeed.

"Well, if he discovers and isolates a network leak faster, his company gets safer and stronger, right?"

Sure, but what would change for him *personally* if he was the one who successfully made his company safer and stronger?

"His company would have happier customers."

We still had to dig deeper.

I asked my clients what the payoff from happier customers looked like, and they said, "Happier customers stay devoted to the brand. They create more business and buy more product."

I asked what happened when customers stuck around longer and invested more.

"The people responsible for that added success get rewarded."

How? Did they have any stories to back that up?

"Sure. One of our clients was so excited by their IT lead's application of our software that they doubled his resources, and he was able to hire six new staffers. He won the top productivity award last quarter." The passion story was getting clearer with each step of the conversation.

I challenged my clients to describe what all those benefits might mean to this award-winning IT guy, someone they'd never even met and had only heard about from their customer. They painted a picture of a user who, once he'd onboarded our software solution, looked great to his boss, made the whole team stronger, got a new title on his LinkedIn profile, and was asked to speak at the upcoming Black Hat event in Las Vegas. I asked what this IT guy's executives thought of his efforts, and they said, "They love him. They want to keep him around, make sure he's happy." Boom—there's the passion.

With 10 minutes of conversational digging, we discovered why our software mattered on a personal, human level. Instead of touting technical merits alone, we now had a passionate story to bring the superiority of our security software to life. We started with "Please buy our software" and wound up with "Our new software can help you become a more valuable asset to your company."

I want to be clear that we never promised our audience they'd get raises or be asked to speak at a conference just because they bought my client's software. We didn't mention new job titles or adoration from company leadership. Those elements were a vital but *internal* guide to understanding the viewer, for personalizing our corporate story, based on what would be most beneficial and inspiring for customers.

And because I was the person going out to tell this new and improved passion story to audiences all over the country, I got to witness their positive responses.

Paint the Passion Picture

A great talk paints a beautiful picture for your audience, a vision of success in a brighter future they can easily achieve thanks to their time with you. Paint the right picture, make it inspiring and inviting, and your listeners will actively want to climb inside that enticing frame.

My friend Michael is a real estate agent in Chicago. He believes the key to selling a house is to help clients imagine that they were always destined to live there. He walks them in the door and quickly gets his clients to picture their family and belongings in that home. His buyers start to think, "Ah, the TV goes on that wall. My kids do their homework by that big window. Our bed will look so good in this room! Our friends are going to love having cocktails on this patio." Once the clients see themselves happily living and thriving in that space, they become passionate about the home, and the offer gets written.

Your talk's content works exactly the same way. Demonstrating passion for your topic helps the audience picture their own success through your solution. As you speak about the value of your brand and its capabilities, you want to help them begin dreaming of a better tomorrow through your storytelling. The more skilled you are at painting that vision of success, the more colorful and dynamic their mental picture becomes. Add splashes of passion, excitement, color, and energy. Your passion compels their passion, which then motivates them to take action on your message. They can't wait to begin turning the picture you've painted into their new reality.

This is how the world's most successful brands approach corporate storytelling. Companies like Microsoft, Adidas, Starbucks, LG, American Express, General Mills, and eBay all speak from and about passion before speaking a word about their products. They capture our imaginations first and our wallets second. They speak to our hearts before they speak to our heads. It is important to understand the difference and why we should always market to the heart before the head in every talk we give, because the head is rarely the best place to market your product. I'll show you the science behind that assertion in a moment.

Let's say you have been asked to speak about last quarter's growth numbers at a user group conference. It's not the sexiest topic, but there's plenty of opportunity to add your own personal passion even in this driest of deserts. Rather than simply laying out statistical reports, ask yourself what the numbers in those reports represent and why they should matter to your audience. You can't just offer numbers; you must paint a picture that helps them see themselves in those numbers and understand how each metric affects their jobs or lives. Numbers speak to the head; passion speaks to the heart.

You might share how last quarter's growth or contraction was a point of personal pride for you or one of personal regret. If last quarter's figures were disappointing, what does that say about the industry you share with the members of your audience? What does it say about your clients or the unique ways your company partners with them to serve a common market? Or maybe last quarter's numbers exceeded expectations, and you're proud to have played a part in that success. You feel your team's hard work paid off, and you are excited to be an integral part of a thriving industry despite economic challenges.

Head messaging versus heart messaging is also defined by where you focus your passion: toward yourself or toward others. If numbers are up, and you played a role in that success, bragging about it plays to the head through ego. But bragging about the brilliance and hard work of *others* plays to the heart through generosity and communal celebration. Which do you think is more likely to connect with and inspire your audience? If numbers are down, head and heart messaging work in the opposite direction. Blaming others for the bad quarterly report is mental justification, while taking the blame yourself and sharing the lessons you've learned conveys humility, humanity, and a desire to improve—it speaks to the heart.

Say your breakout session is about ways to support remote workers during a global pandemic. Thousands of articles and hundreds of podcasts have already addressed the new work-from-home reality, so how do you add your own passion around such a widely covered and well-explored topic? It is not enough to simply fill your script with company metrics or publicly available statistics others have published. You must paint a passion picture of where work from home will take us and why we should look forward to a future of more productive, creative, and flexible workforce opportunities.

As you explain emerging remote employee performance data, look for opportunities to apply personal perspective and human experiences that will bring that data into focus. What struggles with remote teamwork have you overcome, and what inspirational victories have you heard about from others? Create a compelling picture of what is possible in our new hybrid work world. Take time between statistical measurements and process graphs to share your passion for customers who have used your solution to achieve amazing results that improved lives and delivered success. Your passion for transforming the reality of being a remote worker will inspire your audience to embrace an uncertain and potentially frightening future. Your vibrant picture can speak to their hearts instead of their heads.

The Science of Shared Passion

The science behind heart-versus-head marketing is one of emotion over logic. Inspiration and motivation are driven by feelings, occurring primarily through gut reaction rather than academic analysis. Most brands speak to the head using measurement, documentation, sales records, and selfish victories. This is counter to the science, which suggests that a corporate story directed at the heart will almost always trigger emotions and a passionate reaction that imbue the brand with deeper meaning for the audience.

Uri Hasson, associate professor in the psychology department and the Neuroscience Institute at Princeton University, studies a fascinating human phenomenon called brain coupling.[23] Hasson's research shows we can get others to experience something that we ourselves have experienced through the stories we tell. The brain of the person telling the story—you—and the brains of those listening to that story—your audience—synchronize

---

23 Hasson, Uri. "This Is Your Brain on Communication." TED. 2016. https://www.ted.com/talks/uri_hasson_this_is_your_brain_on_communication.

around shared narratives and similar human experiences.

For example, we all buy groceries. We all work. We all look for love. We all eat, sleep, walk, read, watch TV, play with our children, travel, sing, and dream. Long before speaker and audience meet, our stories have a commonality that creates a foundational connection between the storyteller and the listener.

If you just explain what your product, service, or brand does, you are not creating an opportunity for natural human-to-human brain coupling. But when you follow each data point or deep-dive explanation of your product with a personal story or passionate investment, you synchronize your shared experiences with those of your listeners. I highly recommend Uri Hasson's excellent 2016 TED Talk for a deeper trek through how we share memories and knowledge through "common code that presents meaning."[24]

When we deliver a public presentation, each word we speak and text bullet in our PowerPoint starts its journey in a small segment of the audience's frontal lobes called Wernicke's area, a region of the brain identified in 1874 by German neurologist Carl Wernicke containing motor neurons involved in the comprehension of speech. We call it "the lizard brain," the main language-processing system that hears information as it is delivered and translates "blah blah blah" into coherent meaning. Our audience's Wernicke's areas hear our words and see the numbers and decode everything in our talk, and then ... nothing. That's it. Our listeners process, and they're done.

Our job as a speaker is to move those decoded messages along, guiding them safely out of our audience's Wernicke's areas and into their full processing spectrum in the prefrontal and frontal mantles. The next stop is the insula, another tiny wedge deep in the cerebral cortex that controls emotion and empathy. When you add passion to your talk, minimizing corporate speak and including personal perspective, your audience's insulas connect your experiences with moments they have experienced in their own lives. Now your corporate story starts sounding familiar.

As your audience's tiny insulas process each bit of data into a

---

24   Hasson. "This Is Your Brain."

recognizable story, that data transfers to the front of their brains, where creativity and executive function take place. Numbers and statistics come to life in each frontal lobe, and your beautiful picture starts bursting into color. Instead of simply crunching statistics in their heads, your listeners are suddenly sharing your experience in their hearts.

The technical term for this shared communicative process is "orality," more commonly known as oral tradition. Since the dawn of our species, humans have been telling stories around the campfire. Much later, we told them around Grandmother's table in Phoenix. Glossophobic or not, storytelling is in our DNA.

The written word was first popularized in Sumer, near the Persian Gulf, around 3,400 BC. But despite more than 5,400 years of advances in technology, science, and extensive global interaction since the Sumerians, orality remains the primary method of human communication. Multiple recent studies across six continents show that person-to-person storytelling is still the dominant mode of communication regardless of constantly increasing rates of global literacy and the rise of the internet. It's bigger than television, books, and even social media. With rare exceptions, we get our information from one another. Simply put, you were born to speak in public.

Recognizing your innate evolutionary ability to tell a story includes recognizing your audience's desire to hear you tell it. The science of shared passion for good storytelling means you just have to get out there and offer the value your listeners already crave. Deliver the value, and you create the connection.

Scott Dinsmore, founder and CEO of Live Your Legend, inspired millions with a 2012 *Forbes* article called "The 7 Pillars of Connecting with Absolutely Anyone."[25] With full deference to Dinsmore's genius, I offer a paraphrasing of his pillars to help bring out the passion in your corporate storytelling.

---

25   Dinsmore, Scott. "The 7 Pillars of Connecting with Absolutely Anyone." *Forbes*, 2012. https://www.forbes.com/sites/theyec/2012/04/25/the-7-pillars-of-connecting-with-absolutely-anyone/?sh=1e8051ef3419.

Pillar 1: Care Why You're There

If you don't care about the people you're trying to connect with, they'll know. When you care, you communicate. When your passion comes to the fore, it brings out passion in others.

Pillar 2: Offer to Help

Everyone needs help and has something to learn. You have the power to change a life for the better when you personalize your talk and share your passion.

Pillar 3: Pay Attention

You can't help someone you know nothing about. Do your research, and learn who your audience is and what they need from you. Share your story because you share their common passion and goals. Pay attention to them, and they will pay attention to you.

Pillar 4: Find Connections

Turn a lecture into a conversation by making your talk about your audience instead of about yourself. Sharing your passion starts with prioritizing the listener's passion and what connects you to them.

Pillar 5: Persistence Pays Off

The more you speak in public, the more chances you're given to add passion to your talks and the more audience members you can reach. Success doesn't come all at once; it's added drop by drop until the heart overtakes the head, meaning you learn to speak instinctually from personal experience rather than from your data points. Take time, care, and effort in every talk you give, and the passion you get back from your listeners will speak for itself.

Pillar 6: Your Audience Is Your Friend

You only make friends with people you allow into your personal narrative. Be a friend to your audience, and they will offer their friendship in return through more investment in your talk and in your brand.

Pillar 7: Be Unforgettable

When you involve yourself and your passion in your talk, you extend the message, speak with more dimension, communicate more clearly, and achieve greater authority and "stickiness." The better you become at speaking *with* your audience rather than *at* them, the longer your impact will last and the deeper your message will reach. To quote businessman and politician Carl W. Buehner, "They may forget what you said—but they will never forget how you made them feel."[26]

---

26 "Carl W. Buehner." BYU Speeches. Accessed June 25, 2022. https://www.speeches.byu. edu/speakers/carl-w-buehner/.

EILEEN SWEENEY

Philanthropist | Executive | Global CSR Expert
CEO and Executive Producer at Humankind Partnership

"Picture this ..."

If a picture is worth a thousand words, what are a thousand words worth? It can feel as if storytelling is always runner-up to a good picture, but good storytelling is, in fact, a verbal picture. And when we put story and picture together, we are better understood, more tangible, and more effective communicators.

Start with a picture: finite, complete, and unchanging. Storytelling fills in the edges, creating the "before" and "after" of that image. A good story explains, colors, and makes sense of any picture, going beyond the tangible to transport and inspire your listeners.

In a corporate setting, pictures often creep into storytelling through logos, a font, or a piece of equipment, visuals that can either distract from or add to the storyteller's message. If they compete, the audience focuses on the image instead of the story. Good storytellers weave the image into the story, painting a larger picture and commanding complete attention.

The glory of storytelling is in how it moves and shifts, explaining nuance and delighting an audience in ways a picture alone can never do. A moving picture is wonderful. A moving story is truly wondrous.

CHAPTER ELEVEN

FROM CORPORATE SPEAK TO HUMAN CONVERSATION

In Chapter Two, I shared the current Wikipedia definition of "corporate speak" as "the tone associated with large corporations, consultants, and governments using unnatural and opaque language that often creates tedium and lack of clarity. Corporate speak makes meaning and intent unnecessarily difficult to understand, crushing passion and natural conversation." It's time to start removing corporate speak and replacing it with more relaxed, organic, and personal communication that's in your own voice and from the heart. This strategic swap will instantly make you a better speaker. Then it will make you a better corporate storyteller.

Commit to "Remove and Replace"

If this "remove and replace" strategy is so important and beneficial, why don't more speakers apply it to their talks? Because it takes longer to craft personal, meaningful content than to simply cut-and-paste. Turning a corporate message into a connective message requires extra time and attention compared to regurgitating standard talking points and industry metrics. It's simply easier to pull existing phrases and published numbers from a website or white paper, then turn them into your script. Our jobs are demanding, free hours are scarce, and we prioritize expedience. But, as I keep saying, nothing gets sold until the story gets told.

Replacing corporate speak with human conversation takes commitment. It also takes a willingness to bring others into your preparation process. You don't have to discover multiple personal stories on your own; ask a customer or colleague how your product or service has affected them or their own customers. Encourage a team member to describe how using the product has altered your firm's status quo in positive ways. Discover what others are doing differently thanks to your solution, if they'd buy it again, and why. The personal answers you receive will inspire the communicative content in your talk, leading to more organic storytelling and more successful, connective presentations.

Consider this paragraph about printing press ultraviolet (UV) curing and how it might transition from corporate speak to human conversation:

> This new UV drying system is equipped with electronic power supplies that allow the UV lamps to switch to standby mode while the substrate is being retracted. As the web starts moving forward, the UV ink-drying process switches back to the set drying power in a few milliseconds, reducing the energy required by the UV drying system by 50%.

There's a lot of corporate speak here. Industry professionals will understand every word, of course, but it's still just an explanation of a process, with nothing personal to lock the story in. Let's "remove and replace" some of that corporate speak and see what happens:

> Our new UV drying system lets you switch the lamps off when you aren't using them, cutting the cost of every job you run by 50%. Your operator just touches a button, and the UV system goes into hibernation. Then, the moment you need UV drying again, touch the button, and you're back on in milliseconds.

Think about what a difference that's going to make in your power consumption and the extra profit margin on every job you run. This is a huge change from the way you're handling UV curing on your press floor right now.

Here is another example of how typical corporate speak makes a simple message more complex than necessary:

Your organization will thrive with continuous services, profitability, and lower risk. We deliver innovation faster and earlier, through more consistent functionality, using research to create unbeatable value. Wherever you are on your path, our modular services and methods, carefully fitted to your industry and line of business, help you get to the next destination.

Every word makes sense, but this is a mess of corporate jargon with no personalization or human touch to create value or connectivity. Time for "remove and replace" to work its magic:

You've built excellent capabilities that serve your customers so well and that keep your brand in the lead. You're profitable. You get great press. Now it's time to take that next step. Where do you start? First, you have to lower your risk. Second, you have to innovate faster. We want to partner with you on both. Our research shows multiple ways that we can bring you even more value, more modularity, and more consistency. If that gets you excited—like it gets us excited—we can start right now. Today. We've got the plan; you just tell us when you're ready to roll.

Once you begin applying this "remove and replace" effort in your own scripts, you'll notice how often both you and your audience are being hamstrung by corporate speak. Wherever your phrasing gets bogged down by unnatural and opaque language that creates tedium and lack of clarity, replace it with personal references and natural conversation that reveal your passion.

THE CEO AND THE SENSOR

I received a call from a longtime client with an interesting challenge. His massive multinational Fortune brand had pulled out of a powerful conference, but their very popular CEO had been offered the lead keynote slot. In order to accept that offer, the company was required to be a top-level sponsor and exhibit at the event. This was tricky since their brand no longer produced any of the technologies that had been their reason for exhibiting in previous years. We had to create an original story from whole cloth.

I was brought in to help address multiple conundrums. First, what could we show in our enormous Diamond-Level sponsor booth? Second, what would we say to support the CEO's keynote? Third, how could we be relevant and influential at an event where we weren't viewed as a thought leader? We didn't have anything to sell or any hard data to drive attendees to our product demos. With no corporate speak available to us, a world of storytelling was ours for the taking. We decided to offer an experiential, inspirational, and aspirational vision of every attendee's role in creating a more connected future.

The Internet of Things was just starting to tip from primarily machine-to-machine interactions into potential for machine-to-people and people-to-people opportunities, what was becoming known at the time as the Internet of Everything. As personal technologies advanced and proliferated, the number of data connections was exploding exponentially. Capturing, organizing, and applying those trillions of new pieces of data would be thrilling and would give us a better understanding of ourselves and the world around us. Our superheroes were sensors. They certainly weren't a new technology, but most people in our audience didn't realize just how small sensors had become, how cheap and plentiful and ubiquitous they were, and what pictures they could paint.

Rather than drone on about company metrics or percentage industry growth, our CEO showed a tiny sensor on his fingertip. Those in the front row could barely see it. We helped everyone imagine where those sensors would fit into their lives—in clothing that could measure performance or perspiration, in basketballs to measure the number of hours a teen spends active on a court rather than passive on a game console, or in wine bottle labels to ensure peak quality, stable shipping temperature, and improved distribution. We lightened up on the data and doubled down on placing the audience inside our story, making them the stars of our big picture and letting them touch and feel the better tomorrow they themselves would build.

My favorite piece of this highly personal, zero-corporate-speak story centered on personal fitness devices. They were still relatively new but quickly gaining popularity and prominence on the wrists and in the hearts of users. Our brand didn't design, build, or sell fitness trackers, but we showed each visitor how they could use the technology on their wrists to personally contribute to the global community—and how our brand was providing the network backbone to make that shared contribution possible.

Beyond statistics like heart rate, steps walked, stairs climbed, and calories burned, personal health *devices* became their personal *connection* to the Internet of Everything. Users had valuable information to share, anonymously, with health-care providers. Individual information remained private, but aggregate mass data from millions of devices could come together to create a meaningful, illuminating view of wider public health realities. Every person at that event was given a bright and beautiful vision, and while it was explained through technology, they were transported by how we were collectively and creatively improving their day-to-day realities. With over 180,000 people in attendance, there wasn't one who didn't connect with our inspiring corporate story.

Instead of selling a product, we were sharing passion. We connected patients to their physicians, the health-care industry to the public interest, and lower insurance rates to better lifestyle choices. It was all very personal, meaningful, and aspirational, a mutually beneficial future where a fun and affordable technology could support longer and healthier lives. No corporate speak, just human, connective corporate storytelling.

Here's another example of cutting corporate speak in order to create a more connective story.

Personal Communication for Personal Responsibility

A colleague reached out to me with an interesting and potentially risky proposal. His consulting firm was representing a client that serves a market stuck in an endless cycle of discord and stagnation. Brilliant industry players from four key market sectors all agreed on the big vision and end goals but had spent more than two decades infighting, hesitant to cooperate, and unwilling to play nicely in one another's sandboxes. This inaction was preventing their own industry and a planet of frustrated customers from achieving their shared vision.

The idea was to write a manifesto effectively slapping the entire industry playfully but firmly on the wrist. It would argue that if these four sectors didn't get their you-know-what together, and soon, the entire market would pay a severe price. I was intrigued.

My client couldn't achieve their goal of unity and alter the market's thinking through corporate speak; this story had to be highly personal. Instead of focusing on the technology, which everyone already knew and understood, we focused on what the technology was capable of achieving—but *only* if all four players could stop their foolish bickering and finally get on the same page.

That was the risky part. We had to gently accuse each player of how they were short-changing both their own sector and the other three sectors by not living up to their end of the bargain. And we would directly challenge their tendencies to point fingers at the other three. Nobody was safe; everyone deserved critique.

Our story had to originate from, and continually return to, the positive. Every time my client would slip into industry terminology and metric storytelling, we pulled it back to more human examples of alliance and divergence. That meant pulling out chunks of equipment-focused content and replacing it with personal statements from those who had directly suffered and strained under industry delays. Avoiding unnatural and opaque language, tedium, or lack of clarity, we laid out precisely what each sector player could do right now, today, to begin rebuilding trust and move the ball downfield.

Industry response was enthusiastic. While a few took umbrage at our accusations, most embraced the wake-up call and suggestions for a redirect. We took the ugly image of product-centric, fiscally driven, myopic corporate attitudes and instead proposed a transformation that reminded the market why they wanted to do what they do in the first place. This more personal and less corporate vision showed how much more value they could create as partners than as adversaries.

Choose Human Language Over Corporate Language

As you approach your next talk, seize every opportunity to speak from the heart instead of the traditional corporate playbook. Skip the acronyms. Get rid of the buzzwords and "verbed" nouns. Remove and replace the jargon and manufactured complexity with language you'd actually be comfortable using in conversation with a friend.

Don't get me wrong; your audience wants to hear the fine details of your software. They expect a deep dive into your dashboard and to see the latest metrics and percentages. But ultimately, they need to be inspired by your talk, and corporate speak does not inspire. Adapt that corporate speak into natural communication, with clear and compelling passion for how your software will deliver significant personal and professional change. Help them easily see how each metric and percentage will make their jobs easier and streamline their daily efforts.

Simply put, corporate speak detracts; clarity and natural conversation connect, compel, and motivate. Share a good corporate story, one human to another, and the value comes shining through.

DAVE ARLAND

Consumer Marketing Leader | Trekkie | Vintage Car, TV, and Radio Collector
Founder and President of Arland Communications

To be a good storyteller is to know how to capture your audience, to get them to tune in to see the colors and pictures, and then to reveal the twists and turns. A good story can surprise you with the details you remember and the little things that stick with you. You might be drawn in by a cutting-edge innovation that created a new product, or by the surprising beginnings of a humble household staple.

Last week I turned a knob and fired up the 68-year-old RCA color TV in my living room. It weighs almost 250 pounds, and it took more than five years of electronic restoration to return it to its original glory. The dim, colorful, 15-inch screen works best in almost complete darkness so that reflections are minimized. You can almost picture it in your head, can't you? This TV is a story in its own right. Watching it now is like staring back through time, like it just left the production line in Indiana and ended up in my home, ready to glow back at me in the darkness and share its stories.

In 1954, this TV cost as much as a new Chevrolet, and just two hours of color programming per week were available to viewers (only on RCA's NBC network). Add in a few twists and turns, like the maneuvering by RCA to slow down their competitor's lead and the later licensing program that encouraged a flood of overseas color TV sets from new companies, and the story of my 250-pound beauty makes it so much more than just another old television.

Like a vintage RCA, a great story is more than a single beam of electronics hitting just one color of phosphors on an antique picture tube. It's the sweep of colors that brings to life the stories of the world around us.

CHAPTER TWELVE

SCRIPTS: FRIEND AND FOE

AFTER MORE THAN TWO DECADES AS A PROFESSIONAL SPOKESMAN and presentation coach, I've learned to simultaneously view scripts as both friend and foe. "Friend" because a strong script can help a speaker to organize and craft a solid corporate story, guiding the preparation process and focusing value-driven content. "Foe" because, once the values of a strong script have been leveraged, speakers often continue to rely on them as a crutch or memorize the content, leading to automaton-like recitation.

Writing a strong script is critically important to delivering a strong talk. Scripts are your friend when they properly serve two equally significant masters. First, a strong script helps to get thoughts and ideas on your topic out of your head and onto paper or screen. Very few speakers are able to successfully "wing it" and still produce valuable storytelling, reliable audience investment, and an on-time performance. There's a marked difference between knowing your stuff and knowing you'll remember all your stuff, in order and on schedule, when the occasion arrives. Even if you spend your workdays talking about what you do and why you do it, that storytelling takes on added significance once you are asked to deliver an "official" talk. Strong scripting bridges the gap between knowing what you want to say and trusting yourself to say it correctly, consistently, and within the allotted time frame.

Second, a strong script helps put your story into logical structural order. Your script is a treasure map, walking you step-by-step through your talk's trajectory, helping you place each concept and segment in the correct sequence. The map begins with your promise of exciting value to come, then leads through a series of shared challenges, discovering solutions and proofs of concept along the way that build on one another, driving the listener toward their destination of a call to action and your "X marks the spot" treasure of personal or professional payoff and next point of contact.

Strong scripts are easy to follow and easy to speak. They tell a compelling corporate story, and guide both you and your audience every step of the way through the journey of your talk. A strong script is a friend when it serves your goals, your story, and your viewers.

Yet even the strongest script can transition from friend to foe if it sticks around too long and isn't set aside in favor of relaxed conversation and confident control of your message. Many speakers don't trust themselves to deliver their talk correctly without that script in hand, on a monitor, or committed to memory. Knowing when to stop leaning on your script—to accept your knowledge of the story and your ability to tell it—is every bit as important as writing a strong script in the first place. Do not let your friend turn into your foe.

Notice how I keep using the word "strong" when describing a script? That's because a weak script becomes your worst enemy. Where strong scripts support and propel both speaker and listener to success, weak scripts undermine your ability to tell a great story and confuse or disappoint your audience. The wrong script will turn your potentially powerful topic into a waste of time, painful to deliver and inviting glossophobia. There is nothing worse than a speaker desperately trying to make sense out of a chaotic, disconnected grocery list of data points as viewers struggle to keep up and question their decision to attend.

Intimidating as it sounds, the wrong script for your talk is usually worse than no script at all. Here are a few strategies to support your writing efforts and lead you to write the story you actually hope to tell.

Expand Your Outline

I mentioned that we would revisit the final graphic from Chapter Seven, "Creating Thickness." As a simple baseline and first skeletal structure, this chart can start out spare, then expand and adapt as you draft, write, and rewrite the complete script for your talk:

SECT.	ELEMENT	TIME (26 minutes)
1	Welcome and Setup	00:00–00:30
2	Value Proposition	00:30–1:30
3	Personal Introduction and Expertise / Your Why	1:30–2:30
4	Agenda	2:30–3:00
5	Challenge One / Solution One	3:00–6:00
6	Demo One	6:00–8:00
7	Proof of Concept / Value Restatement One	8:00–9:00
8	Challenge Two / Solution Two	9:00–13:00
9	Demo Two	13:00–14:30
10	Proof of Concept / Value Restatement Two	14:30–16:00
11	Challenge Three / Solution Three	16:00–19:30
12	Demo Three	19:30–22:30
13	Proof of Concept / Value Restatement Three	22:30–23:30
14	Restatement of Value Proposition	23:30–24:00
15	Call to Action	24:00–25:00
16	Wrap-Up and Sign-Off	25:00–26:00

Figure 12.1 Baseline sample structure for a presentation

With all the elements of your talk clearly laid out, it now becomes easier to address them, one by one, and ensure nothing gets accidentally missed. Time frames help to focus and limit the quantity of your content, where you dive too deep in one section and speed too quickly through another.

From here, you can begin enhancing your outline with additional details such as key targets and takeaways, specific calls to action, or dedicated callbacks to your opening value proposition. These can serve as inspiration during your content development process and are also useful when sharing your outline with teammates:

SECT.	ELEMENT	TIME (26 minutes)
1	Welcome to Las Vegas Next generation of EV battery science Location-based renewables	00:00–00:30

SECT.	ELEMENT	TIME (26 minutes)
2	R&D time frame and delivery speed Analyst storytelling Customer satisfaction Structural improvement / consistency	00:30–1:30
3	Me and my job Why I love what I do Ashden Award / Green Power Leadership Introduction to our team	1:30–2:30
4	Agenda—step-by-step value	2:30–3:00
5	Wider adoption Range and weather LI limitations SS/SSB breakthroughs	3:00–6:00
6	CATL + SK deployment 2021	6:00–8:00
7	Panasonic India Tie back to frame two payoffs	8:00–9:00
8	Entry cost Plant development Asia v. NA Architecture / thin film X-ray imaging	9:00–13:00
9	Malvern Panalytical walkthrough	13:00–14:30
10	IHS Market report Tie back to frame two payoffs	14:30–16:00
11	EV vs. hybrid charge time Consumer adoption rates by region Analytical instrumentation	16:00–19:30
12	In situ lab + synchrotron demo	19:30–22:30
13	Tesla/Ford/VW applications	22:30–23:30
14	Restatement of frame two value proposition	23:30–24:00
15	Battery Day tickets Jeannie keynote 8:30 tomorrow Lot B ride-along GEV white paper	24:00–25:00
16	Final reminder of what is possible Encourage participation in RAMP study Invite meeting scheduler Thank you (audience, team, industry)	25:00–26:00

Figure 12.2 Added detail to flesh out the baseline presentation structure

Create the outline that serves you best, focusing your intent and guiding each piece of the story you write.

Write Your Own Script

My next recommendation is that you write every script yourself. In my experience, the scripts most likely to succeed are the ones crafted by the speaker, in their own voice and natural communication style. The scripts most likely to fail are written by someone other than the speaker who will deliver the talk. This is not an indictment of anyone's script-writing abilities; often, the person writing the content is intimately familiar with a product's granular details and elemental structure, perhaps more so than the person who will eventually deliver the talk. But when others write your script, your audience can tell, and not in a good way.

Just as it is more difficult to successfully communicate in a language you are not proficient in, it is always harder to successfully deliver a talk written in someone else's words rather than your own. As we detailed earlier, this is an especially common risk for executives, who often have so little available time in their calendars that outsourcing communication is de rigueur. Technically savvy junior staffers are deployed to write scripts for their higher-level bosses, and the results tend to be disappointing.

There are notable exceptions. For example, political speechwriters are highly trained to learn the natural delivery style and linguistic idiosyncrasies of their employers. They have funding, time, and extensive access to study a speaker in fine detail in order to tailor vocabulary, phraseology, and speech patterns to that individual, as if they wrote their own content. This is rarely the case in corporate presentations or those delivered by most employee presenters.

On occasion, a client will hand me a script written by their marketing or product lead, and, from the first word, it just feels wrong in my voice. Their language is not my language; their cadence is far from my own. In order to internalize my client's message and imbue it with my own passion,

I have to make their script into my script. I urge you to do the same any time someone else writes the script for one of your talks.

Practice and Then Let Go

We will assume you have written your own script, one that solidly supports your topic and confidently tells the story you plan to tell. Now it's time to learn that content in preparation for your upcoming talk, and to learn it just enough so your script remains a friend without slowly devolving into your foe.

Practice makes perfect. Some speakers worry about over-practicing, but I find that, for most of us, it's a problem we don't have the luxury of experiencing. More often, our calendars allow for too little preparation rather than too much. If you are a rare exception, consider that a gift rather than a burden. Take all the time you can to become highly familiar and comfortable with your script. Internalize it, record yourself delivering the talk, and watch your performance for clues to potential improvement. Present to others on your team or to your family and solicit their valuable feedback. Then, when you know the content and feel in control of it, and while your script is still your friend, PUT IT AWAY. Yes, I am yelling. Because this is a crucial step in the preparation process that many speakers fail to do.

Your script becomes your foe the moment you know its content but continue to cling to it like a life preserver. Remember, your script does not tell your story—you do. Once you have written your thoughts down in tangible form, organized them into a strong narrative, and learned the content, your script has finished serving its purpose. Tuck it in a drawer and keep practicing from your knowledge of the topic, communicating from the heart instead of from a memorized document.

Whatever topic you have been asked to speak on, you likely already know it inside and out. Under normal circumstances, you can tell your solution story in your own words, at any time, without a script, to any client or colleague. But, once a talk is "formal," others will be watching and listening, and glossophobia starts to creep in. You suddenly worry you might stumble, forget an important point, or won't satisfy expectations. This is why speakers fail to set their scripts aside, using them as safety nets, sacrificing personality and relaxed delivery in order to get every word perfect.

Despite popular opinion, memorization is not your friend. Numerous studies show that memorized text stifles communication and suppresses connection and recollection.[27] [28] [29] When you recite from memory or read your script off the page or screen, you run the risk of regurgitating content *at* your audience instead of communicating *with* them. This is a foe you do not need.

You know what you want to say. And you have slides to cue you along the way. That's enough. Put down the script and tell that story in your own natural cadence, even if it varies from the exact words you wrote. You'll free yourself to adapt as you go, interact with your audience, incorporate them into your talk, and add passion to your more free-form storytelling.

Perhaps you worry that, if you don't follow your script to the letter, you may mistime the delivery. True, dumping the script means you may run short or long, but ask yourself if that really matters. (Remember the 3%–8% rule?) If you run short, you can always add another personal perspective or extend your call to action and conclusion. Better yet, give your audience a bit of time back to make a call, say hello to a friend, or get some fresh air before the next scheduled session. If you were scheduled to speak for 30 minutes and finish in 25, your audience will be delighted by the bonus break.

If you find yourself running long, that is a perfect opportunity to leave your audience wanting more. Bring the session to an end, let them know you still have lots of additional value to provide, and offer an invitation to set up a next point of contact. If you have to wrap quickly and cut

---

27   Orlin, Ben. "When Memorization Gets in the Way of Learning: A Teacher's Quest to Discourage His Students from Mindlessly Reciting Information." *The Atlantic*, 2013. https://www.theatlantic.com/education/archive/2013/09/when-memorization-gets-in-the-way-of-learning/279425/.

28   Meade, Lynn. "21. Delivery Methods—Which One Should I Use?" University of Arkansas. Advanced Public Speaking. Accessed June 25, 2022. https://www.uark.pressbooks.pub/speaking/chapter/delivery-methods/.

29   Fruciano, Mike. "Why Memorizing Your Speech Is Bad." Effective Presentations. Accessed June 25, 2022. https://www.effectivepresentations.com/blog/memorizing-speech-bad/.

something, the 3%–8% rule suggests it was likely something your audience would not have remembered anyway—no real loss. I promise you will never accidentally forget the most meaningful points of your presentation.

Avoid Endless Rewrites

A few words on rewriting. I have seen countless speakers waste gobs of time rewriting and rewriting, overthinking and worrying. They can't help themselves, endlessly making their scripts different but rarely better, right up to the moment they walk on stage. If you find that your script is feeling more like a foe than a friend, return to your outline as the guideline for your talk. Discard the corporate speak in favor of personal stories and human passion. Your next draft may not hit every target perfectly, but your personality will shine through, and the content will start to feel friendly again.

Rewriting does not always strengthen a story, and often makes a story weaker. Be sure that each rewrite is an actual improvement in communication and clarity rather than just another set of words that effectively say the same thing. Each hour you spend rewriting is another hour you delay learning your script and another hour before you can set that script down to rehearse without it. If you're going to make a change, make sure it's worth the time and not just one more round of busywork.

Set a permanent marker date in your calendar for when you will complete the script and begin to practice it rather than continuing to adapt it. Ideally, your script should be finalized and locked in at least five days prior to your presentation. This allows two to three days to learn and internalize that content, then another two to three days to practice delivery with friends and colleagues—without your script—in order to make final improvements before facing your audience.

Create Prompts to Support Your Storytelling

Even without your script comfortably in hand, you still have a variety of reliable technologies available to support your storytelling as you deliver your talk. Slides can also be friends or foes, acting either as helpful visual stimuli or unworthy distractions that make your job harder. Confidence monitors and teleprompters are excellent tools when occasionally glanced at for cues, but you shouldn't be reading full sentences or paragraphs. Notes or cards on a lectern can offer the same support in smaller spaces or lower-budget speaker environments.

When creating your PowerPoint slides or speaker notes, do not load your monitor or index cards with long passages and extensive bullet points, effectively recreating your script on your slides to read verbatim. An audience knows when it's the script doing the talking instead of the speaker. Reading off the slide hamstrings your performance and is disrespectful to your viewers since it's so clear they could just as easily read your content on their own time.

Better corporate storytelling requires whittling each idea in your talk down to its core essence to create short, easily digestible prompts. I recommend crafting cues between three and five words, just enough to spur your next thought with a quick glance at the monitor or your notes before returning to eye contact with your listeners. The more your eyes are on your audience instead of on your slide or script, the more connection and shared communication you'll offer.

Say this is the opening scripted section of my topic:

> Research does not see the booming auto-buying years of the last decade returning until the middle of the 2020s. We could see stagnant sales through 2024 due to the pandemic's effects, economic conditions, and even a shift to more remote work environments. But even as sales remain tepid, we can expect to see far more EVs buzzing around our city streets throughout this decade-long progression and technology development time frame.

If I include all these words on my slide, I will spend my entire talk reading them off that slide or my note cards instead of connecting with my viewers. I'll be regurgitating rather than communicating. Instead, I want to break each sentence in that opening into short cues that easily guide me through my content:

- No boom like last decade
- Stagnant through 2024
- Pandemic—economy—remote work
- More EVs on city streets

I know my topic. These cues give me just enough information to ensure I hit every point with only a brief glance down at the monitor or index card to keep me on track. Then I'm quickly back to my audience and our shared conversation. I'm also free to adapt in real time, speaking from the heart, and using whatever words come to me in the moment.

Here's another example for simplifying a large piece of scripted content into bite-size cues:

Sleep apnea remains a pervasive and prevalent challenge, yet eight out of every 10 patients suffering with apnea remain undiagnosed. This can result in serious health risks, including high blood pressure, stroke, chronic heart failure, or even death. People struggling with obstructive sleep apnea must be diagnosed, begin effective and reputable courses of treatment, and dedicate themselves to complete and compliant therapy. These requirements offer even more challenges. Some patients don't adapt well to sleeping with CPAP equipment. Many abandon therapy, leaving them susceptible to, and at increased risk of, detrimental health effects.

All important information, but nothing that needs to be said verbatim. I can easily be prompted by a few short bullets on my monitor:

- Pervasive and prevalent
- 8–10 undiagnosed
- High BP, stroke, CHF
- Diagnose and treat
- Compliance challenges
- Abandoned CPAP

These few guiding prompts are all I need to tell my story. I may use different words each time, but the communication will be so much more compelling than if I just read the full script off the screen.

Strong scripts are friends that help you arrange your ideas and align them into strong corporate storytelling. Weak scripts are foes that do not deserve your loyalty, memorization, or close adherence. Start by writing a strong script in your own voice, then happily set that script aside when the time is right.

─ HEIDI KETTENRING ──────────

Vocalist | Stage and Screen Performer | Voiceover Artist

I perform a Karen Carpenter concert show, accompanied by expert backup singers and musicians, playing to sold-out houses across the country. We're sharing 40–50-year-old lyrical stories with nostalgic audiences who adore the music but may have forgotten the meaning behind the words they know by heart. My job is to make those beautiful, powerful songs new again and to help our guests feel and experience them as if for the very first time.

As a stage veteran, I know I can make a pretty sound. But I'm on that stage to bring my own passion and perspective to established storytelling. I watch guests take their seats, expecting to simply listen and float inside the comfort of a known commodity. As we open the show, our audience smiles, bobbing their heads in rhythm, singing along automatically in fond recollection.

Then something slowly changes as these melodies they've known so long begin to take on new life. As I personalize each lyric and connect it with each listener, they suddenly hear these stories with fresh ears. Smiles and sways turn into surprising emotion and revelation.

My favorite audience members are those I can tell didn't even want to come in the first place. "The Carpenters? Really? Okay, sure." They sit up and start to lean in. They thought they knew what to expect, but these stories reach them, bring them back, and reignite their hearts.

Richard and Karen Carpenter told their remarkable stories from 1969 to 1983. When I was a child, they made me want to sing. Now I get the joy and magic of creating my own versions of these beloved stories for audiences young and old, for those hearing the Carpenters' legacy for the first time or for the hundredth, but in fresh and wonderful ways.

CHAPTER THIRTEEN

SLIDES ARE STORYTELLERS

THE TERM "DEATH BY POWERPOINT"[30] IS CREDITED TO ANGELA R. Garber. It was first widely shared, unironically and without humor, by Robin Harris in a 2010 "Storage Bits" op-ed, then republished and disseminated by ZDNet following a PowerPoint ban by then Brigadier-General Herbert McMaster. Harris reported on McMaster's 2005 assertion that bad PowerPoint presentations shared the blame for military failures in Iraq and technical disasters like NASA's Challenger explosion as they missed the science or misled the analysts viewing those slides.

As the author suggests, "Give a man a hammer and everything looks like a nail. PowerPoint is a hammer. It does some things well and others—such as presenting complex ideas—poorly, no matter how gifted the presenter. There are many ways to engage an audience with minimal text … and one of the best is with a story." [31] Harris's core assertion was that "PowerPoint is a tool for presentation, not discussion. In a multivariate world, we need more discussion, not less."

Yet PowerPoint not only persists; it continues to dominate. In fact, it remains an expected part of virtually all public presentations. If you are reading this book, chances are PowerPoint is the only presentation program you are completely comfortable using. This is even more impressive considering the advanced age of this relatively unchanged technology. How many other 35-year-old applications still show such unchallenged

---

30   Garber, Angela R. "Death by PowerPoint." Small Business Computing. April 2001. https://www.smallbusinesscomputing.com/software/death-by-powerpoint/.

31   Harris, Robin. "Death by PowerPoint." ZDNet. April 2010. https://www.zdnet.com/article/death-by-powerpoint.

command? I can only think of the combustion engine, a technology likely to cede its leadership in the coming decade. In a world that changes technologies by the hour, where six months old means four months out of date, PowerPoint continues to thrive.

In 2010, General James N. Mattis, Marine Corps, Joint Forces commander (speaking without PowerPoint slides at a military conference in North Carolina) said, "PowerPoint makes us stupid."[32] With all due respect, I disagree. Stupid PowerPoint makes us more stupid; smart PowerPoint is a valuable and powerful tool for enhanced communication.

How ubiquitous and dominant is PowerPoint? The software was created in 1987 by Robert Gaskins and Dennis Austin for Macintosh computers. Three months later, Microsoft bought PowerPoint for about $14 million, their first major acquisition and an early investment that paid off quite well, thank you very much. As Microsoft's Windows OS grew, so did PowerPoint's worldwide dominance in market share, which reached 95% by the late 1990s. That astonishing leadership holds to this day and shows no sign of retreat. Even Keynote, Apple's attempt at recovering a bit of what they sold off so long ago, only registered a 0.1% market share in 2017.[33]

Love it or hate it, odds are you use PowerPoint and use it liberally. PowerPoint may have negative connotations, but leveraged properly (smart rather than stupid), your slides can provide exceptional corporate storytelling while helping your audience internalize and process your topic's undeniable value.

Every slide you put on the screen during your talk can either support your brand story or undermine it. The right picture can be worth a thousand words, while the wrong picture can make your words fall flat. Well-crafted PowerPoint bullets and diagrams can solidify an idea or metric for your audience, but badly-crafted PowerPoint visuals cause confusion or distraction.

---

32   Bumiller, Elisabeth. "We Have Met the Enemy and He Is PowerPoint." *New York Times*, April 26, 2010. https://www.nytimes.com/2010/04/27/world/27powerpoint.html.

33   G., Dipika, Caitlin O., Kaitlin D., Nicola H., Megan B., and Shannon L. "Who Are the Biggest Players in the Global Presentations Industry and What Is Their Share? (By Number of Users, Revenue, Etc.)." Wonder. July 15, 2017. https://www.askwonder.com/research/biggest-players-global-presentations-industry-share-by-number-users-revenue-etc-ee0fb6843#.

Fundamentally, a great story shouldn't require any pictures or bullet support of any kind in order to succeed; just ask General Mattis. A strong speaker delivering a strong message is enough to share value and passion and to connect with an audience without the need for visuals to shore it up. But this is rare. Most speakers incorporate slides into their talks. And those slides deserve and demand the same focused time, effort, and care as your scripted, spoken content.

Scott Adams, creator of the *Dilbert* comic strip, was a bit less forgiving when he coined the term "PowerPoint Poisoning" in 2000 ("As you can clearly see in slide 397 …").[34] We all know that sinking feeling of a speaker droning on and on through a deck of 30, 40, 50, even 60 slides as we wonder if it will ever end or if we will remember anything we've been shown. Most of us are more appropriate with our slide decks, but we still need to follow a few simple strategies guiding the creation of smart visuals.

Conduct a web search, and you'll discover countless articles, lectures, and blog posts offering PowerPoint "best practice" dos and don'ts. Some slide design rules are repeated everywhere; others are more subjective and targeted. What follows here is a bit of each, my own unique set of strategies gleaned from over two decades watching thousands of presentations, witnessing what a good set of slides can do for a speaker—and, more importantly, what they can't or shouldn't do.

Most professionals believe they can build a strong, supportive PowerPoint presentation. Most professionals are wrong—not because we don't know how to use PowerPoint but because we don't know how to use it *correctly*. And because we don't know what we don't know, we suffer from overconfidence in our ability to build a good slide.

As with a script, a slide deck can be your friend or your foe. Smart slides will guide you through each stage of your talk with subtle cues and foundational support for core values and key content assertions. Stupid slides will compete with your message, confusing viewers and detracting

---

34   Adams, Scott. "PowerPoint Poisoning Comic Strips." *Dilbert*. August 16, 2000. https://www.dilbert.com/search_results?terms=Powerpoint+Poisoning.

from an otherwise empowering talk. In a nutshell, a smart deck makes you a better speaker; a stupid deck makes your job far harder. Let's get smart.

You Are the Primary Storyteller, Not Your Slides

Humans are visual creatures. When we are presented with an option to either listen to or read the same information, we are likely to prioritize reading. Multiple studies on what is known as learning styles have shown that visual learning is, in fact, dominant, and perhaps superior, compared to auditory learning. This presents a conundrum for any speaker; if our audience will get more out of reading our message off the screen than hearing it spoken out loud, what is the benefit of giving a presentation in the first place?

Other publications suggest there is little or no difference between auditory and visual learning and that the learning styles assertion is in fact a "neuromyth" with no scientific evidence or empirical data to suggest any such thing as a visual or auditory person.[35] The Learning Styles Challenge is a collection of five underwriters who have collaborated to offer a $5,000 prize "if any person or group creates a real-world learning intervention that takes learning styles into account—and proves that such an intervention produces better learning results than a non-learning-styles intervention."[36] That prize has yet to be claimed.

Yale University's Poorvu Center for Teaching and Learning argues that "multiple modalities can assist all students regardless of proposed learning style."[37] According to research by Richard E. Mayer in ScienceDirect,

---

35 Rousseau, Luc. "Let's Scrap the Neuromyths: No, You Aren't a 'Visual' or 'Auditory' Person." The Conversation. July 15, 2020. https://www.theconversation.com/lets-scrap-the-neuromyths-no-you-arent-a-visual-or-auditory-person-141957.

36 Thalheimer, Will. "Learning Styles Challenge—Year Eight—Now at $5,000." Work-Learning Research. August 4, 2014. https://www.worklearning.com/2014/08/04/learning-styles-challenge-year-eight/.

37 "Learning Styles as a Myth." Yale Poorvu Center for Teaching and Learning. Accessed June 25, 2022. https://www.poorvucenter.yale.edu/LearningStylesMyth.

"students learn more deeply from words *and* pictures than from words alone."[38] This suggests that the correct balance of a strong storyteller supported by smart visual stimuli combine to offer the most complete opportunity for engagement, connection, and message retention.

The key words in that last sentence are "correct balance." This is where many speakers miss the mark by letting their slides take over the story, subjugating their own session leadership and ability to connect with the audience to bad graphics and paragraphs of on-screen text, aka stupid PowerPoint. Because a fellow human will likely read before they listen, that speaker is deliberately ceding authority to their slides each time any new visual pops into view. Mid-sentence, the audience's eyes and attention instantly transfer from the speaker to the monitor, prioritizing the latest piece of stimuli. Unless the content on that slide is meant to steal focus, the presenter has willingly and deliberately interrupted their own storytelling.

The guiding rule in any talk is that the story comes from the speaker, not the slides. Any image, bulleted text, number, graph, or on-screen quote you share with your audience is only worthwhile if *it follows you*, not the other way around.

The Myth of Multitasking

Humans pride ourselves on an incorrect assumption that we are masters of multitasking. According to studies shared by *Forbes*,[39] *Psychology Today*,[40] and Cleveland Clinic,[41] as well as other academic and medical studies, our ability

38 Mayer, Richard E. "The Promise of Multimedia Learning: Using the Same Instructional Design Methods Across Different Media." *Learning and Instruction* 13, no. 2 (2003): 125–139. https://doi.org/10.1016/S0959-4752(02)00016-6.

39 Lohrenz, Carey. "The Shocking Truth About Multitasking in the Age of Distraction." *Forbes*, June 15, 2021. Accessed June 25, 2022. https://www.forbes.com/sites/forbesbooksauthors/2021/06/15/multitasking-in-the-age-of-distraction/?sh=114933e74918.

40 Napier, Nancy K. "The Myth of Multitasking." *Psychology Today*, May 12, 2014. https://www.psychologytoday.com/us/blog/creativity-without-borders/201405/the-myth-multitasking.

41 "Why Multitasking Doesn't Work." Cleveland Clinic. March 10, 2021. https://www.health.clevelandclinic.org/science-clear-multitasking-doesnt-work/.

to multitask is a myth. We are, in fact, task switching, an effort that is proven to be less efficient, lead to more mistakes, and deplete both focus and energy.

When we ask our audience to hear us speak while also reading and integrating new information from our slides, we are forcing them to task switch. One moment, the speaker holds 100% of the listener's attention. Then a new slide appears, and the speaker sacrifices half of that attention to PowerPoint. But is that slide content compelling and valuable enough to warrant the switch? Are your on-screen graphics, charts, or text bullets so vital that it's worth giving up your previously unchallenged human connection with the viewer?

And it gets worse. Because humans prioritize visual over auditory stimuli to such a high degree, studies suggest the actual split may be closer to 70/30 or even 80/20.[42] And the more content a speaker loads onto a slide, the longer it will take for the audience to read and process that slide before returning to the speaker's story.

If an attendee needs 30 seconds to absorb what you show on the screen, they won't truly hear or understand anything you are saying to them during that time. You might just as well stop talking altogether to read the slide along with your audience. Until your viewer has finished processing your on-screen content, your speaking becomes a distraction from your own PowerPoint. This is an incorrect balance and a losing corporate storytelling strategy. When we are the primary storyteller, that's smart PowerPoint. When our slides are the primary storytellers, that's PowerPoint making us stupid.

Consistent Storytelling

If you are saying one thing, and your slide is saying or showing another, you and your PowerPoint are in direct competition with one another. Beyond task switching and divided authority, your audience gets confused

---

42   Moisala, Mona, Viljami Salmela, Emma Salo, Synnöve Carlson, Virve Vuontela, Oili Salonen, and Kimmo Alho. "Brain Activity During Divided and Selective Attention to Auditory and Visual Sentence Comprehension Tasks." *Frontiers in Human Neuroscience* 9 (February 2015). https://doi.org/10.3389/fnhum.2015.00086.

processing two separate messages simultaneously. Your spoken message should lead, and your on-screen message should follow, always saying the same thing at the same time. Even small text variations can derail a great message.

Sometimes, you might want your slide to take authority for a moment. Just make sure that choice is deliberate rather than accidental. A good picture really can be worth a thousand words, and a change of focus adds visual interest and variety for your viewers. If you decide to let your screen do the talking, give that occasion full focus and specificity. Tell your audience why you are deliberately redirecting their attention to the slide and away from you, explaining exactly what they are looking at and why it matters:

> Take a look at this graph—it tells you everything you need to know. This line shows the speed of electric vehicle adoption, and that line shows the speed of EV charging infrastructure investment. You can see the problem, right? This line needs to go up and that line needs to come down, or we'll be selling internal combustion engine vehicles for another fifty years.

Because the visual tells a better story than words in this instance, you are choosing to switch up the authority. Instead of your slide being in service of you, you are momentarily in service of your slide. Your audience understands the role reversal, and confusion is avoided. Once that visual story has been conveyed, you are ready to retake control and bring the attention back to you as the speaker.

Slides Are Not Scripts

Too much information on a slide is worse than too little. If you feel compelled to overload your slide with text, charts, colors, and bullets, it is a clear sign you don't know what is most valuable to your audience or what story you are trying to tell. A busy screen shows a lack of focus and confidence in your own learning objectives. Simplify your slides, clarify the primary benefit, and get rid of the clutter so the truly valuable content stands out.

At the same time, your slide is not a place to type out your entire script. Nothing is more detrimental to a speaker's storytelling than an overreliance on PowerPoint in order to get through a talk. And if your audience can read the slides as you recite them, they have no need for you.

When an audience watches a presenter constantly reading paragraphs off the screen, they shut down and lose faith in the message and the messenger. Slide after slide overloaded with massive chunks of text puts viewers to sleep. Their patience and attention fade, and they start to fear the barrage of information coming at them: the very definition of death by PowerPoint.

Smart slides are designed for your audience's benefit, not your own. Learn your content, and practice until you are comfortable and in control of it, with as little reliance as possible on your deck. In the previous chapter, I suggested truncating your paragraphs into short, three- to five-word cues that successfully guide you through your content while keeping you connected to your audience. Jump back a few pages, and remind yourself how to do this effectively.

One Big Idea Per Click

Build your PowerPoint so that each slide focuses on only one big idea or value payoff per click. This strategy allows your audience to hear and view a single important benefit, understand and process it, and internalize it for their own payoff without distraction or competition. As you tell the story of that single big idea, your targeted and specific slide is working to keep your audience in that particular moment. Do not force them to absorb too much visual information all at once. If your slide shows multiple points of focus or asks the audience to incorporate multiple values, split that slide into two or three instead.

Show your PowerPoint deck to colleagues, and ask them to tell you what they first notice in each slide when it pops up. Ask what they feel is the most valuable piece of information on the screen and why. Ask if the slide's message is immediately obvious, clear, and compelling. If what they see and what you want them to see aren't perfectly aligned, fix that slide.

Assess how long it takes for those trusted colleagues to process that slide before answering your questions. The longer it takes for them to discover the key content and how it creates benefit for them, the longer it will take your audience to return to your voice and storytelling. Five seconds is excellent; 25 seconds is problematic. Simple, immediate visual value serves both you and your listeners best. If text takes too long to read, trim it down or get rid of it. If an image or chart isn't immediately understandable, replace it. If the single primary value proposition doesn't leap out and announce itself, refocus and redesign. Simplicity is key.

Clean Up Your Text

Once your text is added to the PowerPoint, proofread again and again for basic spelling and formatting errors. Again, I encourage you to find a trusted family member or friend to be your second or even third set of eyes before you show any slide to an audience. Misspelled words may seem benign, but they demonstrate carelessness and a lack of attention to detail. The subconscious message for your audience is that if you are careless in building and delivering your own talk, you may be equally careless in how you handle their business needs.

Most of the time, a misspelled word on the screen is subconsciously corrected in the audience's minds with no foul or effort. But if the error is egregious or changes the meaning of your message, you could lose credibility. If the error is accidentally humorous, a serious talk can turn funny for all the wrong reasons. Here is a recent bullet point misspelling that didn't get caught in advance:

"Work it like you moan it!"

When I saw that pop up on-screen, it took me a moment to realize what was going on. First, the word "moan" is fairly amusing in its own right, especially when seen out of context. Second, I had to figure out that the speaker actually meant to type the word "mean"—work it like you *mean* it! How could they not have noticed and corrected that typo earlier? Third, I took an extra moment correcting that sentence in my mind in order to process the speaker's original intent. Fourth, it took a bit of time to parse the meaning of that new phrase: "Work it like you mean it!" What was the speaker trying to say to us?

As I was doing all these mental gymnastics, the speaker had been moving forward with their content, but I (and the rest of the audience) hadn't heard a word. We had just spent 15–20 seconds processing a simple on-screen spelling error, one small letter that accidentally dropped one very large speed bump in the presentation.

Syntax is equally vital. Poor grammar, odd word arrangement, and badly formed sentences pull a listener out of your story. Instead of connecting with your next big idea, the audience temporarily focuses in on slide text that just doesn't read correctly to them for some reason. Your storytelling fades to the background as your viewers try to work out why your on-screen text feels odd or disjointed. For instance,

*"Do not use vectors when you can't
open or see unseen boxes."*

Huh? Three ideas, clunky syntax, not/can't/unseen ... this is going to take a moment for an audience to unravel and comprehend. Here's another mind-twister:

*"Fit gaskets where gasket overlap
won't impede connection."*

At first that seems to make sense ... or does it? Maybe a second read, just to be certain, or even a third. Meanwhile, the speaker is two or three sentences along in their script, and the audience has missed it. Clarity counts. Help your attendees quickly read and process your intended message, stay in the moment, and always be ready for whatever you say next.

Once the right text is in place, be certain it's presented in the best possible way. Look for balance between words and images, and leave proper space around your text boxes so they don't look sloppy or rushed. Text that overlaps or pushes right up next to an image feels cramped and uncomfortable. Shoving text too close to the edge of the screen also reads as a mistake.

Always justify your alignments. Misaligned bullets, random spacing, or line quantity disagreements look "wrong" to an audience, even if they can't instantly recognize why. When things don't square up, they gently trigger our subconscious, universal desire for balance and uniformity. It is subtly frustrating to see one of three bullets inconsistently aligned or capitalized:

- 2019 Revenues = $136.866 billion
- 2020 Revenues = $139.537 billion
- 2021 Revenues = $141.262 Billion

Pay attention to numbers of lines of text. For example, if you have three sets of text that work together to tell one story, get that text on the same number of lines across all three:

The head is rarely the best place to market or to increase customer success.	Numbers speak to the head; passion speaks to the heart.	Heart vs. head marketing prioritizes emotion over logic.

Figure 13.1 Uneven numbers of lines of text

Four lines then two lines then three lines feels wrong to the viewer. Stretch or contract your text boxes or edit your text to make them match. This is a simple change, but appears more pleasing and balanced for your viewer when it hits the screen:

The head is rarely the best place to market or to increase customer success.	Numbers speak to the head; passion speaks to the heart.	Heart vs. head marketing prioritizes emotion over logic.

Figure 13.2 Creating symmetry with the same number of lines of text

Next, resize your line separation spacing for easier on-screen reading. Lines that are too tight together are uncomfortable and hard to read. Lines that are too far apart appear separate instead of flowing as one single idea:

Choosing the best welding helmet for the specific job is very important. The wrong lens can cause short- or long-term retinal damage.

Versus

Choosing the best welding helmet for the specific job is very

important. The wrong lens can cause short- or long-term

retinal damage.

Versus

Choosing the best welding helmet for the specific job is very important. The wrong lens can cause short- or long-term retinal damage.

Simple fixes like these can make a big difference. They ensure your on-screen text is clean, clear, instantly recognizable, and easy to process.

Graphics, Charts, and Images

One of my mentors used to say, "Get rid of the unimportant so the important can speak." Any graphic, chart, image, schematic, or diagram you show on a slide has to easily and confidently prove valuable and accessible to your audience. If they won't immediately get it, or they may not benefit from it, you want to get rid of it.

Visuals are often added to PowerPoint decks for the wrong reasons. Sometimes a visual is a favorite image of the company, mandatory or standard in all presentations, but offers no connection for attendees. Some graphics find their way into slides based on the intimate expert knowledge of the speaker without considering if the audience will view it from a position of equal expertise. And sometimes an image is included for no other purpose than to add color or liven up a dull slide. Assess each visual honestly and objectively; if you're not absolutely certain your attendees will find it inspiring or beneficial, dump it.

Many diagrams and flowcharts create confusion by burying their big payoff behind excessive numbers and complicated on-screen processes. Lines going every which way, icons spilling across the model, and x- and y-axes measurements that confuse more than they excite all indicate a challenging graphic. Here are some confusing graphic examples:

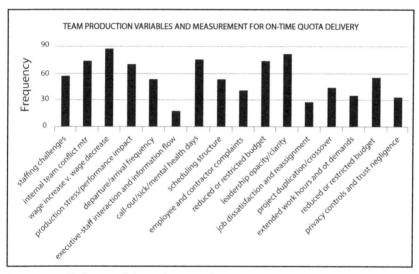

Figure 13.3 Challenging slide graphic example 1

Consider the substantial time an audience will need to read, process, and internalize the extensive text on this slide. And while they're doing so, how much spoken content they'll miss as the presenter presses on in their script.

Try the same assessment with this graphic:

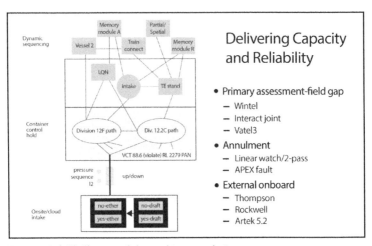

Figure 13.4 Challenging slide graphic example 2

Imagine the audience listening to a speaker when this slide pops up on the screen. Even an expert will have a hard time extracting concrete benefit in this complicated flow. What's most important to the viewer? Where is the big payoff, gold nugget, or exciting change buried in all this detail?

And how long would you take to fully understand everything happening here?

Figure 13.5 Challenging slide graphic example 3

Could you absorb it all in 20 seconds? 40 seconds? Either way, whatever the speaker says while you decode and assess value in this slide will be lost and useless.

Simplify your graphics for the benefit of your listeners. If a visual is required to include so much information in order to prove your point, walk us through the graphic to illuminate the undeniable benefit. For example:

> This dashboard shows full stack optimization across all your network applications. Don't worry about all these rack components or data routes; just look at what's happening right here in the center, in red. That is what matters for you. See all these outer elements converging across these connection points? That's your processing power. That's where it all pays off for your business!

When it comes to on-screen graphics, consider yourself a film director, pointing the camera or aiming the spotlight right where you want to direct your audience's attention. You can maximize focus on graphic elements that deliver peak value, and you can downplay less meaningful graphic content that your company insists you share but that you'd prefer to leave out.

You can (and should) apply this same director strategy to excessive text bullets. If a slide includes too much text that you're required to show, help your audience to focus in on the most important bullet and minimize the rest. A lengthy laundry list of text choices only confuses the viewer; guide them straight to their most valuable option on that list, visually and audibly:

> Here you see fifteen different coding options for delivering secure access to end users. My favorite is number six—this is the one I use because it's the fastest and easiest to deploy. You can use as

Prioritizing, Positioning, and Placement

The biggest, brightest image, graph, or chart on a slide will always be the first thing your audience sees. Be sure it deserves that level of attention. Imagine this is the first time you've been shown that graphic; what does it tell you? Is it clear and compelling? Does it create any confusion or question of value?

Next, critically assess the graphic to determine whether it powerfully supports or unnecessarily conflicts with your spoken message. Will the audience instantly grasp its meaning, or will it take them a few extra moments, causing them to miss the next part of your story?

If you use multiple images on a single slide, do those images cooperate and build each other up, or do they compete and reduce each other's impact? Should one take precedence over another? Is it imperative that your audience understand image A in order to understand image B? Once again, seek input and honest feedback to ensure your on-screen story is as smart as your spoken story.

Placement of graphics on the slide is also important. Many speakers work from the top down or from left to right, building a message piece by piece and leading to the big payoff at the bottom or right side of the screen: "This, plus this, plus this, leads to that, ergo VALUE!" That doesn't work. Humans process value in order, from the top down or center out; whatever they see first is what they assume is your most important message. If you place that main message further down the slide, your audience misses your intent. The big value payoff belongs at the top or in the very center of the screen, then support for that value goes below or around the outside: "VALUE! Thanks to this, this, and this."

Size, color, and brightness are keys to perceived content value. A larger image will always grab attention before a smaller image, and a more colorful graphic will always overshadow one shown in grayscale. Once you've designed your slide, close your eyes for a few seconds and then open them as if the slide just came on-screen; where does your eye go first? What leaps out, and what do you barely notice? Do you process elements in order, or do you have to backtrack (bottom to top or right to left) in order to take it all in or understand the story? Graphic layout really does matter.

Color Counts

Companies spend thousands and even millions to create brand colors and slide deck color guidelines that tell a specific story and keep speakers from going too "freestyle." You can and should assert the same focused control in your own deck. Smart use of color in your PowerPoint theme makes your slides dynamic and consistent and helps your audience to prioritize primary versus secondary value. Create a color strategy that supports your brand and adds visual interest to your corporate story.

Choose a simple but deliberate palette, and stick to it across your entire deck; if your company colors are orange and blue, your primary messages or key concepts on each slide should be offered in those colors. Don't go too simple or too wild with your text and graphic colors; slides that are entirely black and white are uninspiring, severe, and have a soporific effect on your audience. Too much color on a slide, or too many different colors, can be overwhelming, distracting, and unprofessional.

For example, a speaker representing Intel will use corporate-approved hex color code #0071c5 to match their brand logo, then toss in a second shade of blue and a bit of green for contrast. If that speaker then throws in a random orange header, giant yellow question mark, and bright pink URL, their deck begins to look chaotic and confusing.

Color tends to take authority over black or gray, so use your limited palette of bold and consistent colors to draw the eye. If your key colors are red and blue, your most vital and valuable text and graphics should be shown in those power colors, not in black or grayscale. Use those more muted options for your subtext and secondary graphic elements.

If you have two different angles to your talk, one corporate and one personal, consider putting all corporate content in one color and all personal content in another. This is known as color theming because the color informs the audience as to what perspective is being offered in each slide:

> Here you see the end user in gold and the hacking organization in purple. Wherever those colors converge in this flowchart is an opportunity for cyberbullying, or exposure and eviction.

Each color shows one side of the equation, and your audience easily follows along with every word of your story.

Fonts Tell Stories Too

When it comes to font selection, clean and professional are always your best bet. A bit of research will guide you to the fonts that are widely considered best practice and easiest to read. It's important that they remain readable across a variety of platforms, programs, and distances—remember, the last row of your audience may be 100 feet away from your screen. Arial, Helvetica, Calibri, Garamond, Century Gothic, Futura, Tahoma, and PT Sans are all considered standard, recommended fonts for use in your slide deck.

Be careful with overly creative, playful, or even silly fonts; while they might look adorable to you, that is an opinion that may not be shared by your attendees. Curlicues, cursive, emoji, etc., could be jarring in your slides, negatively affecting your credibility and content.

In most instances, limit yourself to one or two fonts across your entire slide deck. Three or more is unprofessional. Multiple uses of a single font (altering size, boldface, and italics, etc.) is ideal, but there is nothing wrong with adding a second font for visual variety. Ensure the two fonts complement rather than compete with one another; for instance, a corporate Avenir combined with a playful Chalkduster would be jarring and misaligned.

Fonts can dictate mood. In most talks, your intent is to deliver with authority and expertise, so you'll want to choose a highly professional and clean font that reflects that tone. A more personal talk might be better served by a slightly less corporate font, one that is gentler, with softer edges, and offers a bit of personality. If a talk is loaded with personality and comedy, a severe font will create a disconnect between the speaker and the text on their slides. Choose the font that reflects the mood and feel of your spoken story.

Most documents utilize first-level title text, then smaller, second-level subtitle text, and finally, third-level body text. These different sizes convey structure and priority, ensuring your biggest value proposition on each slide stands out from everything around it. As with the color directive above, whatever point provides most value for your audience on each slide belongs in title text, supported by subtitle or body text in smaller and less vibrant fonts, used conservatively and in limited amounts so as not to distract from your main objective.

Pay Attention to Logos (and Footers)

Scour your PowerPoint to be absolutely certain your logo is consistent in size and placement across every slide. If the logo gets larger and smaller as you move through your deck, or jumps from position to position, even by a few pixels, that's another sign of sloppiness that is easily fixed. Use your slide master to standardize logo size and placement, or copy from slide one and paste the logo onto all other slides so it never moves around as you advance.

Check that you are using the latest Legal-approved logo on every single slide. Sometimes a previously used slide is imported or adapted from one deck to another across months or even years, but the logo doesn't get updated along the way. It can be very risky to accidentally use outdated or unintentionally varying brand logos in different sizes and colors. These can generate raised eyebrows in an audience and legal problems for your company. Standardize your logo, and confirm its use through careful proofing.

How closely do you pay attention to the footer on every slide in your presentation? If you are speaking in 2023, and the copyright at the bottom of your slides shows 2019, you have a problem. Your slides should read current and up to the moment, even if they were repurposed from past PowerPoints. If your footer shows internal information like deck version or an outdated subheading, take those out; you don't want to be giving a public presentation with a deck that says "v4 for internal use only" at the bottom.

You also don't want to be presenting on one topic while your outdated footer shows a different topic. I've seen this unfortunate error many times when a speaker leverages slides from another talk or even from another speaker's deck. The topic is "Creating a Culture of Patient Safety," but the slide footer reads "Continuing Certification for Patient Self-Assessment." Another simple fix that, left unchecked, risks looking unprofessional and careless.

If your slides include a footer for legal and protection purposes, keep it simple and short: copyright symbol, year, company name. Then make sure every slide shows the identical footer. You can easily control this in your master slide.

Avoid Overload: No Death by PowerPoint

How many slides should be used in a 30-minute talk? As a general reference, I recommend one to two slides per minute: 30 minutes = 30–45 slides total. Too few and you can't click often enough, leaving your audience itchy for a change of visual. Too many and you'll need to race through your deck, overwhelming viewers with more text and graphic content than they can possibly absorb in a single session. Forced to choose, I'll opt for too few slides over too many. Fewer slides mean the audience spends more time focused on the storyteller instead of on the screen.

Perhaps you don't have enough graphic or text content to justify that many slides, and you plan to deliver your 30-minute talk with only seven or eight, keeping the focus on you. That's fine, but your audience may crave a bit more visual variety. Try adding a few logo or title slides into your deck that allow you to advance more frequently. You can even add solid-black slides that let your audience know it's time to stop looking at the screen and return their full attention to you. This demonstrates confidence in your story, proving that you and your content are strong enough to stand alone without graphic support.

On the other end of the scale, I've watched speakers deliver a 30-minute talk while ripping through 72 slides. Oof. There really aren't enough facepalm emoji for mistakes like this. In these unfortunate instances, the speaker's deck was almost always lifted or repurposed from another longer talk. They didn't know what to remove so they kept everything in, bludgeoning their poor audience with a ridiculous amount of unnecessary visual stimuli. These speakers rush through their slides in a selfish, machine-gun barrage that undervalues both their viewers and the strength of their own message.

Even in a 60-minute presentation, 72 slides would still be problematic. The smartest audience simply cannot consume and retain this much information in a single sitting. Limit the number of slides, focus them on what matters most to your attendees, and give them just enough on-screen content to keep them engaged without expecting them to process a visual onslaught.

Your Final Review

PowerPoint may be antiquated and oversaturated, but it remains ubiquitous and uncontested. No other presentation application has come close as a valued tool for easy, streamlined storytelling and accessible, cross-platform sharing. Used to its potential, PowerPoint should be a big positive in getting your story told and sold.

Once you've built out your deck, recruit a colleague or two to carefully review each slide from your audience's perspective. Ask them and yourself these important questions:

- ❏ *Does every slide look professional, clean, and dynamic?*
- ❏ *Does anything appear sloppy or rushed?*
- ❏ *Does every image tell a clear and compelling story?*
- ❏ *Do graphics enhance value or create confusion?*
- ❏ *Are text bullets short and focused?*
- ❏ *Is everything easily read and quickly processed?*
- ❏ *Are long sentences or paragraphs required, or can they be cut down or deleted?*
- ❏ *Is there a pleasing balance between text, images, and graphics?*
- ❏ *Does the spacing feel right, or do elements crowd or overlap?*
- ❏ *Do edges of text and graphics align?*
- ❏ *Is color used consistently and appropriately?*
- ❏ *Are fonts standardized?*
- ❏ *Is text formatted to highlight big value concepts over smaller supporting content?*
- ❏ *Is there any chance the audience could miss the primary value on any slide?*

These honest assessments will help you avoid death by PowerPoint and achieve the *correct balance* between speaker and slide. This is how we take a 35-year-old technology and put it to its intended use, in smart instead of stupid ways. My suggestions may sound nitpicky, but a tight, professional, organized deck is scientifically proven to encourage acceptance, demonstrate value, and increase your message retention.[43]

When Things Go Dark

---

43   Klemm, William R. "Organize for Better Thinking and Memory." *Psychology Today*, April 16, 2016. https://www.psychologytoday.com/us/blog/memory-medic/201604/organize-better-thinking-and-memory.

At the start of this chapter, I hinted that a great story does not require any support from pictures or text bullets in order to succeed. A strong speaker delivering a strong message should confidently stand alone, without the need for any visual shoring up.

Now, imagine disaster. Your laptop dies mid-session. Perhaps a frayed extension cord disrupts power or connection to the screen, or someone trips over and yanks out the HDMI cable. What if there was a technical problem in the venue or loss of Wi-Fi connection, or your IT lead accidentally loaded the wrong PowerPoint deck? Could you comfortably continue without your slides? The answer should always be a resounding yes.

The more your presentation relies on slides, the less it relies on you. While slides can strengthen and support your corporate storytelling, they are no substitute for your personal connection with the audience and the passion you bring to a talk. If your deck were to vanish from the screen, you should have no hesitation pressing on without it. The more prepared and confident you are with your content, the more likely you will keep calm and carry on when things go sideways.

CRISTIÁN GÁLVEZ

Moderator | Keynote Speaker | Author

Germans love facts and figures, and German executives often reject storytelling as unnecessary in the business world. They cling to PowerPoints, KPIs, and pie charts for communication success, afraid to simply share their personal experiences without the safety net of data or metrics to help them. I could show them countless scientific studies proving the effectiveness of storytelling; instead, I tell them a story of my own:

Every year, I prepare a pediatric heart clinic's medical team for their annual media appearances. In the corridors and playground, children walk with their parents, towing a so-called Berlin Heart, a small suitcase with a long tube extending into the child's body, keeping them alive. These children live in a hospital, waiting years for donor hearts, each with a tube connecting them to the living world. Then something amazing happens to the lucky ones who survive: They go home with their parents. But the tube remains—no longer in their hearts but in their heads. Subconsciously, the tube still feels like a vital link with the living world even though it is no longer needed to survive.

And so it is with storytelling. The doctors and business experts I prepare for their media appearances cling to tubes of data, a clinic of slides and graphs, unsure how to communicate without them. They have learned to rely on technical PowerPoints that slow them down instead of recognizing that they are, in fact, free to run. Free to share their own beautiful experiences of health and survival without a tube connecting them to facts and figures. I help them remove the tube.

We all have behavioral "tubes" in our heads that once connected us to some sense of survival. When we learn that it is no longer necessary to sustain or define life, we can remove it in order to tell our stories from the heart without towing a suitcase of fear behind us. This is true for the Berlin Heart patients—and for anyone with a meaningful story to tell.

CHAPTER FOURTEEN

PREPARE TO SUCCEED (STORY CONQUERS SWEAT)

A BRILLIANT QUOTE, OF ANONYMOUS ORIGIN BUT OFTEN CREDITED to Benjamin Franklin, says, "By failing to prepare you are preparing to fail."[44] One in a hundred speakers can defy this rule, but the odds suggest that, when it comes to you and your talk, Mr. Franklin was spot on. An underprepared presentation is disappointing for an audience. And if the speaker can't be bothered to put in the time and effort on their own talk, an attendee wonders if that speaker can be counted on to find time or care for their needs as a customer. The more you prepare for your presentation, the more your audience will see and appreciate that investment in yourself and in them.

The Pressure of Performance

Lack of preparation doesn't just neglect the viewer; it also leads to glossophobia. A rush of adrenaline may see us through the first few words or opening slides of our talk, but once that initial spike ends, the crash is inevitable. There is simply no good excuse for stepping on stage and asking others for their valuable time and attention without first investing our own time and attention to perform at peak capacity. Ego in our natural abilities or overreliance on the quality of our product are not excuses for lack

---

44 "If You Fail to Prepare You Are Preparing to Fail." Quote Investigator. July 8, 2018. https://www.quoteinvestigator.com/2018/07/08/plan/.

of preparation; once the microphone goes live, those who don't follow Ben Franklin's (or whoever's) sage advice tend to choke.

Sian Leah Beilock, cognitive scientist and president of Barnard College, gave a TED Talk entitled "Why We Choke Under Pressure—and How to Avoid It" that reveals what happens in the brain and body when we get caught in stressful situations. When you are naturally good at your job and know your topic inside and out, it's easy to feel pre-prepared and fully on point at a moment's notice. But even the best at what they do suffer a degree of performance anxiety, feeling confidence slip away when they are faced with an audience.

According to Beilock, a soccer player with Olympic aspirations, her performance slipped when she realized the coach of the national soccer team was standing right behind her: "In a matter of seconds, I went from playing at the top to the bottom of my ability. Just knowing that I was being evaluated changed my performance."[45] Why does this happen, and what can we do to prevent it?

Beilock goes on to suggest that, while we might spend a lifetime working on our craft, we spend far less time working on readying our minds for the pressure of performance. "Whether we're taking a test or giving a talk, it's easy to feel like we're ready, at the top of our game, then perform at our worst when it matters most." Call it performance anxiety, stage fright, or opening night jitters, but the formality of giving a public talk changes the paradigm for every speaker. Even the most seasoned expert can seize up in the spotlight.

Imagine you and I grab a beer one afternoon, and I ask you to tell me about the topic of your upcoming talk. Because you are good at your job and confident in your subject, you will have no trouble explaining your topic and outlining the challenges and solutions you plan to share and why. Our conversation is casual, informal, and off the record; it's just one friend to another. You can answer my questions extemporaneously with easy authority and speak for an hour without thinking about it. Then, a week later, you step on stage to deliver that exact same information to a

---

45   Beilock, Sian Leah. "Why We Choke Under Pressure—and How to Avoid It." TED. September 2018. https://www.ted.com/speakers/sian_leah_beilock.

conference but without proper rehearsal. Now your talk is official, with far more on the line. Colleagues, strangers, and your boss are watching and listening to every word. I've seen the most confident speakers crumble between that beer and the stress of the formal environment. Context counts.

Some speakers thrive—or believe they thrive—on off-the-cuff, spur-of-the-moment orality. Always assume that you are not one of those speakers. Even if you enjoy public speaking and feel highly confident in its practice, give yourself ample time and opportunity to rehearse. Some speakers worry their talk will become over-rehearsed, diminishing energy or spontaneity and making it sound too canned and forced. While this is certainly possible, most of us don't have that luxury or time. Given a choice between the two, I'd go for too rehearsed over not rehearsed enough any day of the week and twice on Sunday.

As I mentioned earlier, roughly 73% experience some degree of glossophobia, suggesting that three in four of us will falsely critique ourselves as being comparatively "weaker" speakers, and the remaining one in four comparatively "stronger." But "weaker" and "stronger" are subjective terms. There is no uniformly accepted scientific method for measuring these percentages in terms of presenting ability. I've watched brilliant presentations by deeply glossophobic speakers and dreadful presentations by those who consider themselves supremely confident on stage. Almost always, the difference is in preparation. Your natural ability to present is not the determining factor of success; it is far more about your commitment to valuable content, passionate delivery, and dedicated practice that results in a great performance.

There is also no universal path to better corporate storytelling. Your way is the best way. It's the only way for you. We have covered a variety of tips and tricks for increased value, passion, and connection up to this chapter, but the way you'll bring it all together is through practice. Plenty of practice.

Recreate the Live Environment

Unfortunately, most of us never get the opportunity to practice in a similar setting to the one we'll actually be speaking in when that big moment arrives. We feel fine in our homes and offices, speaking in our heads or in front of a mirror. Then we step into the spotlight, and our brain shifts gear; we choke or end up giving a talk that looks and sounds very different from the one we planned. Quality of preparation is as important as quantity.

You have to show your work to others, encourage their honest feedback, and feel what it's like to speak to, and for the benefit of, an audience before actually facing that audience.

Reading your script quietly to yourself off a computer screen is far quicker than speaking that script out loud. Your actual performance will include breaths, pauses, audience queries, and slide advances, all adding to your total session time. What clocks out at 28 minutes in your office can turn into 34 minutes in the spotlight. If your presentation slot is only 30 minutes, you now have a problem. It's a stress you don't want or need. Stand up, speak out loud in full voice, and time yourself with a stopwatch to see how long your story truly takes to deliver.

Get on your feet. Standing will net a very different performance than rehearsing while seated at your desk or on the sofa. Practice in front of friends, colleagues, or family members. If no one is available, record your full presentation on a mobile phone and share that footage with a small, select remote audience. Try to make your practice situation as close as possible to your live event situation in order to close that gap between preparation and the eventual venue.

Use Your Own Words

A sure way to reduce stage fright is to use vocabulary and phraseology that feel comfortable in your mouth. In Chapter Twelve, we discussed why it is always harder to successfully deliver a talk written in someone else's words rather than your own. Corporate speak and unfamiliar language spark discomfort in the subconscious that diminishes relaxed communication. If something feels unnatural in your mouth, it will feel equally unnatural in the audience's ear.

As you practice your script out loud, pay attention to any word or sentence that feels clunky, too corporate, or makes you stumble, then rewrite it in your own organic language. Think of how you would express that idea as we sit around together enjoying that beer. The more casual and comfortable you feel while storytelling, the more relaxed and confident you'll come across to your audience.

Don't Say It if You Don't Mean It

One of my biggest pet peeves is when a speaker tells us how excited or thrilled they are about something without looking or sounding either excited or thrilled. It makes my skin crawl, and it stands out like a sore thumb for its insincerity and laziness. Listen for this gross misstep the next time you attend a talk.

Imagine the poor company that speaker represents. After two years of costly development, representing thousands of expert hours, their presenter stands in front of the media and says, "And now I am delighted to announce the release of Version 7.2," using the same flat, bored, unsmiling delivery as the rest of their talk. Really, you're delighted? You sure don't seem delighted. If you tell an audience you're proud, excited, thrilled, elated, ecstatic, energized, or any such inflated adjective, you have to demonstrate the passion to back it up.

If you tell your audience about something that makes you angry, concerned, frustrated, or frightened, your vocal intent has to demonstrate that you are, in fact, angry, concerned, frustrated, or frightened. If the words and the story don't match up, the moment falls flat. Don't say it if you don't mean it.

This rule is particularly important when you are the one introducing something brand new, say an innovation, news item, or recent product launch. Any first public exposure needs to be slowed down, leaned into, and elevated to the level it deserves. Demonstrate passion in your vocal intent to make that important moment stand apart as opposed to sounding just like everything that comes before and after your big announcement.

When everything sounds the same, you sound scripted and uninterested.

That will invite skepticism and disconnection from your audience, increasing your stress and glossophobia. Practice *in*tent as part of your *con*tent.

Vary Your Tone and Embrace the Pause

Monotonous speech patterns lull both you and your audience into boredom. Practice altering your inflection, ending some sentences up and others down. Change lecturing statements into questions that encourage audience interaction and participation. When you add variety, you stay mentally engaged with your content and keep your audience wondering what's coming next.

Add pauses to your talk, even if you don't need them. We tend to think of pauses as a negative empty space when the speaker is trying to work out or remember the next thing they want to say. But a pause for impact and time to process is actually a positive and powerful tool in your corporate storytelling arsenal. Consider inserting a pause in the flow of content to put special focus on key concepts or to make your audience think or even respond instead of just listening passively.

Numerous studies have touted the power of the pause to improve clarity, enhance connection with an audience, demonstrate confidence, and reduce stress.[46][47][48] Pauses are gold. But many speakers remain uncomfortable with silence, racing ahead in their content or unconsciously filling gaps with "um," "uh," "y'know," "basically," "literally," "believe me," etc.

One of the questions I'm asked most often is how to speak without including these unnecessary, distracting, and stress-producing fillers. The answer is to practice pausing. If you find yourself repeatedly saying "um"

---

46   University of Gothenberg. "Pauses Can Make or Break a Conversation." ScienceDaily. September 30, 2015. https://www.sciencedaily.com/releases/2015/09/150930110555.htm#.

47   Rehn, Alf. "Every Great Speaker Is a Fantastic Pauser—Using Pauses and Silences in Public Speaking." *The Art of Keynoting* (blog). Medium. March 29, 2016. https://www.medium.com/the-art-of-keynoting/every-great-speaker-is-a-fantastic-pauser-on-using-pauses-and-silences-in-public-speaking-84b64f28f070.

48   Dutra, Ana. "The Power of Pause." *Harvard Business Review*, January 5, 2012. https://www.hbr.org/2012/01/the-power-of-pause.

and "uh," that is your discomfort with silence as your mouth races ahead of your brain. Silence is frightening, so while your mind works out what comes next, you feel a need to fill those gaps. This is a bad habit that needs correction. Record yourself speaking and listen for these meaningless interjections. Count them and become aware of their frequency. Notice them as you share dinner with a friend or participate in a Zoom meeting. They are adding to your stress, reducing your confidence, and undermining your authority with listeners.

Remember, a pause can represent power and control rather than weakness. Let your brain work without distraction from your mouth. Think, then speak. Watch others who have made the pause into an art form; you can drive trucks through Barack Obama's pauses as he carefully works out what to say next. Get rid of the worthless filler so the worthwhile part of your talk shines through. Teach yourself to embrace the silent pause. Your stress will decrease, and your audience will escape the verbal detritus of ums and uhs as you process the next valuable piece of content for their benefit.

Banish Nervous Body Language

Confident body language is another tip for reducing presentation stress. Wandering aimlessly around the room as you speak increases your heart rate, while standing calmly with confidence lowers your beats per minute. Practice anchoring as you speak; instead of scuffling your feet or nervously pacing back and forth across the stage, stand strong in one position. Take in the full audience with your eyes alone, using simple turns of the head. Try connecting with each attendee without taking a step. Stability calms the nerves and represents power and authority.

Then, when you transition to your next thought, move to a new position on the stage and anchor there. You can still take in your entire audience, but reducing that extraneous movement will reduce your speaking stress.

If you tend to bounce from leg to leg, swing your legs one in front of the other, or stand with your legs crossed, these fidgets are likely to add tension and agitation. They also make your audience nervous. Minimize unnecessary movement, and allow listeners to concentrate on your story value rather than get distracted by your insecure body language.

What to Do with Those Hands

Hands pose a similar challenge and can also add pointless tension to your talk. There they are, hanging around, not sure where they belong or how to keep themselves occupied. Try holding an object as you present, maybe a wireless mouse to advance your slides, a pen, or a fidget cube. Giving your hands something to do as you speak can release a lot of pent-up anxiety.

Try to avoid hands in pockets, on the hips, or clasped behind the back or in front of the genitals (otherwise known as "the bodyguard" or "the fig leaf"). When in doubt, let your arms relax at your sides. It may not feel natural to you, but it looks totally normal and relaxed to your viewers.

If you have a podium on stage, use it to lean on or as a resting place for a hand or elbow. This will also help you anchor in one spot and prevent wandering, two stress reducers in one. And, if you naturally speak with your hands, as I do, don't stifle that tendency; let them contribute to your storytelling.

Honor Your Worries

Any number of things could go wrong during your talk, so practicing ways of minimizing those risks in advance can do wonders for your glossophobia, building confidence for when it's needed most. Perhaps you worry that your audience won't respond or won't trust or respect your expertise or that your content won't hold their attention. Maybe you worry that you'll say or do something foolish on stage, leave out an important piece of information, or make a fatal error that could result in negative evaluation. These are all legitimate concerns when delivering a talk, and they're all easily dispelled with the right preparation and frame of mind.

In Chapter Five, I asked you to trust that you were assigned to deliver this talk for a reason. You know your topic. You understand the challenges your audience members face each day. You believe in the concepts and solutions you have to offer. You are good at your job. If you weren't, you wouldn't have been asked to give this talk in the first place. That all makes sense, but what about my stance? What should I do with my hands? Is the tone and scale of my voice interesting enough? Why is that lady looking at her phone instead of paying attention to me? Despite our expertise on the topic, we begin to overconcentrate on the wrong things, leading us to under communicate for our viewers.

According to Sian Leah Beilock, we get in our own way by concentrating too much on what we should or shouldn't do or say rather than relying on practice, personal experience, and natural speaking ability, what she refers to as "autopilot."[49]

Here's a simple exercise that proves Beilock's autopilot theory: Close your eyes, clear your head, and focus on nothing but breathing for 60 seconds. Concentrate on how long you breathe in … then how long you breathe out. Feel how much breath you inhale … then how much you exhale. How long does it take to breathe in? Then how much time to breathe out? Count the seconds in … then count the seconds out.

The more you concentrate, the more erratic and forced your breathing becomes. You overcompensate or start to pant. What happened naturally and easily in the subconscious has now grown labored, stilted, and unnatural simply by giving it too much thought, a form of what is often referred to as analysis paralysis (or paralysis by analysis).[50]

As you deliver a public talk, you might be thinking: "Stand still. Stop fidgeting. Fold the arms … No, put your hands in your pockets … No, just let the arms hang down … That feels weird. It's really hot up here. How much time do I have left? The audience is getting bored. Is the microphone

---

49   Beilock. "Why We Choke."
50   Kurien, Rony, Anil Rao Paila, and Asha Nagendra. "Application of Paralysis Analysis Syndrome in Customer Decision Making," *Procedia Economics and Finance* 11 (2014): 323–334. https://doi.org/10.1016/S2212-5671(14)00200-7.

too quiet? Too loud? Damn, that person just got up and walked out. They hate me. I forgot to fix that slide. Did I remember to say that super-important thing? I'm letting my team down. My boss isn't going to be happy. I wish this thing was over. I have to pee." The audience senses you starting to choke, feels your glossophobia growing, and their confidence in you fades as your performance declines.

A valuable tool for reducing this analysis paralysis is to write down your concerns, getting them out of your head and onto paper. If you're worried about the success of tomorrow's talk, try this data download: list any self-doubts running through your brain and rebut each legitimate concern with respect for your innate knowledge and natural skill set:

- ❑ *I know my topic better than my audience does.*
- ❑ *I'm very good at my job—if not, I wouldn't be doing it, and I wouldn't have been asked to give this talk.*
- ❑ *I have information my audience needs and wants.*
- ❑ *I have real value to share.*
- ❑ *I care about my customers and have a genuine passion for helping them.*
- ❑ *They are going to see my passion and expertise, and they are going to trust me.*
- ❑ *It doesn't matter if I forget something—they can easily go back and find that information for themselves.*
- ❑ *It doesn't matter if I wander around—I'll just hold a pen to calm myself down.*

This simple exercise can help get the worries out, stop them from spinning you into a frenzy, and boost your confidence.

Another Argument for the Moment Before

Remember "the moment before" from Chapter Seven, "Creating Thickness?" In that context, it was about giving your audience a moment to connect with you before leaping into the core content of your talk. But you can also take your own moment before you walk out on stage to distract yourself from nervously waiting on the sidelines. It's a fantastic way to prepare for your talk and lower pre-performance anxiety.

As you wait to be announced, pop in your AirPods and dance to a feel-good song. Try humming a favorite tune, repeating a funny tongue twister, or looking at cute photos on Instagram or videos on TikTok—really anything other than cramming a last-minute review of your speaker notes. Stretch, breathe, and get out of your own head. Take that moment before to remind yourself why you do what you do and that you are very good at it.

Anxiety is contagious. If your boss and team are nearby and uptight about the presentation, you are likely to become uptight along with them. Don't allow them to have that negative influence on you and your talk. Get away. Find your own quiet space, leaving others to stew far from you. The same advice applies when you find yourself on the program with other nervous speakers, all sitting around cramming and sweating before their turn. Escape their personal chaos for a moment of your own zen, reducing their opportunity to transmit stress onto you.

Smiles, Everyone, Smiles

You may have heard that smiling is a proven stress reducer. That might sound like faux science, but the studies are extensive and compelling.[51] [52] [53] Even a forced or fake smile stimulates a positive emotional reaction, lowering the heart rate in response to stressful situations. As you practice your content, also practice smiling from time to time throughout your presentation. You're allowed to enjoy yourself and have a good time with your audience while you talk to them.

51   Stromberg, Joseph. "Simply Smiling Can Actually Reduce Stress." *Smithsonian Magazine: Science*, July 31, 2012. https://www.smithsonianmag.com/science-nature/simply-smiling-can-actually-reduce-stress-10461286/.

52   NIH Research Matters. "Smiles Affect Responses to Stress." National Institutes of Health. March 13, 2018. https://www.nih.gov/news-events/nih-research-matters/smiles-affect-response-stress.

53   Paddock, Catharine. "Smiling Reduces Stress and Helps the Heart." Medical News Today. August 1, 2012. https://www.medicalnewstoday.com/articles/248433#1.

A smile demonstrates that you have passion for your topic and for sharing it with others. No one wants or expects a constant, pasted-on smile; that's creepy, not genuine. But if your content is important to you, something you are proud to be a part of and believe can bring value to your listeners, then that is certainly worth smiling about. A few extra smiles will reduce your glossophobia, energize your delivery, and encourage your audience to smile back. Everybody wins, creating more opportunities for a positive response.

Benjamin Franklin (or that anonymous source) understood that the more we prepare, the less anxiety we experience. Each of these small steps can increase confidence and promote relaxation, helping you to become the best possible version of yourself when the time comes to take that spotlight. Prepare your story, and you'll reduce your sweat.

Give rehearsal your full effort and dedication. Time your talk so you know exactly how long it takes to deliver. Use your own words for comfort and natural conversation. Practice in front of others, and solicit their honest advice. Try varying your tone and sharing your excitement, frustration, anger, or celebration. Embrace the pause and concentrate on eliminating unnecessary vocal fillers as you process your next important thought. Relax your arms, anchor in one spot, and add a few smiles to show genuine passion for your topic and your guests. Honor your worries in advance, then trust your own knowledge and ability. Take a moment before your talk to set the notes aside, breathe, stretch, and detox. Prepare to succeed, and let your story (instead of your sweat) fill that room.

A Quick Word About Speaker Coaching

As a professional coach, I am, of course, deeply passionate about speaker coaching and have seen the benefits of this valuable work firsthand. At the same time, I also believe that coaching only works when it is practical, immediately applicable, and uniquely tailored to each individual presenter. When coaching is generic or standardized, or built on hype and motivational cheerleading, it's rarely successful. So how can you tell if the coaching you've been offered is beneficial and worthwhile?

In general, if your company offers you an opportunity for coaching, take it. If you prefer to hire a speaker coach on your own, I highly recommend doing so. Just as an all-star baseball player or Olympic gold medalist still relies on a coach for tiny performance improvements, even the best speakers in the world work with coaches to further improve their onstage delivery. And you should too. But finding the right coach, with the right approach for you, is vital.

Most speaker coaching agencies offer prepackaged, one-size-fits-all courses that promise to give speakers proven, supposed "best practice" skills to increase presentation success. Only humans are not standardized, and one size never fits all. Every speaker is singular, with their own organic, natural storytelling style, mannerisms, and personal preferences. Any worthwhile speaker coach will recognize these realities and tailor their support to your unique needs.

Whenever you work with a coach, whether professional or internal, remember that there is no universal "right" way to deliver a talk; there is no yardstick for measuring what makes your presentation successful or disappointing. Whatever way you choose to deliver value, passion, and connection is, by definition, your "right" way to give a presentation. The right coach will recognize and embrace that distinction to bring out the best in you.

DAVID GIROLMO

Broadway, Television, and Film Actor

Everyone tells stories. *Everyone*. From the first cave dwellers drawing pictures of hunters and horses on the walls of Lascaux or lions and rhinos on the walls of Chauvet, or the simple, incredible hand stencils in Sulawesi, to the most celebrated authors in human history, we have told our stories and broken the silence of centuries in the prayerful hope that someone will see us, hear us, and know we were here. It is a stretch for immortality, a reach to live a little longer.

We tell the stories of our lives because we have to. We are compelled to do this—it's almost a biological imperative. It is the nature of the stories we tell that makes us different and the nature of the stories we consume that defines us.

I've got my own stories, and I do so love to tell them. But my professional life has been all about telling other people's stories. Actors find the author's voice in the characters they play and the director's voice in the way they present that voice/story. The most profound joy in the theatre is to give and take the stage with love for your colleagues and *tell the story* as the playwright and director demand. When their story becomes your story, it's magical.

CHAPTER FIFTEEN

STORYTELLING THROUGH A CAMERA LENS

WHETHER YOUR AUDIENCE IS SITTING DIRECTLY IN FRONT OF YOU or somewhere out there in the digital ether, they are equally committed to your talk. This means you must be just as committed to delivering the value, passion, and connection your viewers are tuning in to receive. The only difference between storytelling in person and storytelling on camera is a small circle of glass, but that small circle can feel like a world of separation. This chapter is dedicated to helping you overcome the *perceived* isolation of hosting a remote session. With a few tools in your belt, you can reframe your negative perspective toward online versus in-person speaking, and learn to communicate to the camera as well as you would to a live room.

As a speaker coach, I hear the same complaint again and again: "Remote events suck!" I get it. We prefer to look our audience in the eye, to see their in-the-moment responses, nodding heads, and raised hands. We like a large stage to wander across and a screen to gesture at. When we present to the camera, we present alone, staring at a monitor and trying to communicate to a cold pane of nonresponsive glass. If 73% of speakers are glossophobic at live events, we become even more so when faced with nothing more than a laptop lens.

Speakers have been delivering presentations both in person and on camera since the public introduction of television in the 1940s. Then in 2020, in-person talks suddenly became impossible, and on-camera delivery became the standard overnight. In January of that year, we were still in the room together, looking into one another's eyes, telling stories face-to-face, and shaking hands the moment we walked off stage. By March, we were entirely alone and physically disconnected, staring into our cameras and missing the familiar feedback loop of a shared environment.

We assumed this mandatory separation would be short-lived, a few weeks or months at most. But a multiyear pandemic changed global corporate storytelling logistics; speaking to the camera became the new normal. Prior to COVID-19, communication and network technologies were already on an eight- to 10-year trajectory toward operational digitization. Work-from-home and work-from-anywhere models were on the rise around the world; the pandemic simply sped up that process, forcing companies to adapt or perish. It's clear that remote presentations are here to stay, and the sooner you embrace the reality of the era we now live in, the sooner you'll become a better remote speaker.

Meanwhile, storytelling has not changed. While delivering to a camera does present certain challenges, numerous technologies have quickly and impressively evolved to make that effort easier and more accessible. Logistics vary, but human nature does not; it will take more than a few years of difficult times to significantly alter 200,000 years of practiced orality. Whether you tell your story in person or online, the guiding principle remains: Nothing gets sold until the story gets told. The tools you've acquired throughout this book are applicable to either platform.

Most speakers view addressing a live room and addressing a camera as two very different endeavors. They're not. In fact, they are the same—with one exception, which we'll get to in a moment. Regardless of your presentation medium, the audience is still right there in front of you, listening, responding, watching, and waiting for the value you've promised to offer. The camera lens is simply an alternative gateway to those same living, breathing humans who used to be in the room and who are now equally invested on the other side of a digital connection.

The exception I mentioned is the loss of our immediate feedback loop, the fundamental interaction of live theater. Speakers and audiences feed off one another, creating an active dynamic that offers clues and propels us through a performance. Delivering to the camera means half that equation is missing. To give a good virtual talk, you must replace the feedback loop for your viewers with added energy, enthusiasm, passion, smiles, and direct eye contact.

This energy boost takes practice and concentration to achieve. It may feel forced or even inauthentic at first, but you are now responsible for both your side of the interaction and that of your remote viewers. Your added commitment reaches through the lens and establishes that meaningful, personal connection with your online audience.

Here are some technology tips and tricks to get you and your camera telling better stories together.

Separate Your Camera from Your Screen

Start by creating a clear delineation between your camera and your computer monitor. When you present to the built-in camera on your Mac or PC, that little lens and your slide deck live on the same pane of glass, leading you to forget the camera and direct all attention toward your PowerPoint. Pop-ups and notices on your monitor create additional distractions that pull your focus off camera. It's easy to forget that a real live audience is out there watching you in real time. And when you look anywhere other than into the lens, it's like turning away from your viewers.

Take some steps to separate your camera from your screen. For example, place small sticky notes on either side of your laptop lens, with arrows pointing inward that read: LOOK HERE! Another strategy is to tie a white string across your screen that creates delineation between the camera above and your content below. Or you could drag your PowerPoint window down, leaving black space between the top of your slide and the lens above. Anything to remind you that your listener is not in your script or slides but up top, watching you speak.

I recommend investing in a separate, dedicated USB webcam that clips to the top of your computer or sits close by on a small desk tripod.

You'll find a wide range of 1080p models under $60 that install in seconds and deliver far better resolution than any built-in laptop camera. Most also include a high-resolution microphone that simultaneously captures cleaner audio than native laptop mics. And because these units separate your camera from your screen, they are easier to focus on and play into.

Maintain Eye Contact

When you deliver a presentation in person, you're constantly scanning the room to take everyone in and connect with as many attendees as possible. Online, your attendees are all gathered together in one single place: that camera. The only way to look at all your viewers is to look directly into your camera lens. If you look anywhere else, you're neglecting the audience, which defeats the purpose of a connective presentation.

Many virtual presenters spend their entire talk staring at the script or slides. Think of your virtual presentation as if it were taking place in front of a live audience—because it is. Constantly looking down at your slides is exactly the same as spending an entire in-person presentation constantly looking down at your confidence monitors or behind you at the projection screen. You would never ignore your audience like that in a conference room, so you shouldn't do it during an online session.

I recommend that you revisit Chapter Thirteen for guidance on creating simple cues that allow you to easily glance down at your slides, gather your next thoughts, and quickly return to the camera. When you maintain your storytelling focus into that lens, you'll compel your guests at home to maintain their focus on you.

This is vital to successful virtual presentations. When you look away from the camera for extended lengths of time, you invite your audience to look away and disconnect as well. Don't give them that invitation. In-person audiences might glance at their phones, but anything else requires that they get up and walk out of the room. Your online audience, sitting in their homes or offices, has more distractions than ever, and all just a click away. If you're looking at your slides instead of at your viewers, it's easy for them to justify task switching in order to check email, answer a text, or prioritize other business while you chatter on in the background.

The way to keep viewers connected with you is to stay connected with them. Look in that camera, and they'll remain focused on your face and content instead of on going to the bathroom or getting a snack from the fridge. Let the audience do those things during the next speaker's session, not yours.

Mind Your Surroundings

Once you decide where you will record or deliver your on-camera talk, step back and view that home or office presentation space from your viewer's perspective. Does it look professional, organized, and credible? Or does it look messy, unappealing, and lazy? Would you be equally comfortable and confident delivering an *in-person* keynote in the exact same setting? Consider that pile of boxes next to you, the messy desk, or the unmade bed in the background—if you wouldn't accept these things on stage at a conference, you shouldn't find them acceptable on camera.

Set up where you plan to record, then turn on your camera and snap a screenshot (Command-Shift-3 on a Mac or Print Screen/PrtScn on a PC). Open the photo and decide if it properly represents the value and expertise your topic and audience deserve. Care in your setting reflects care in the quality and value of your talk. It tells your viewers that you take pride in your job and are equally likely to take pride in your customers and their needs.

You don't have to go to great lengths or expense creating a perfect re-cording environment; just clean it up and minimize distractions. Get rid of clutter, brighten the room, and find a pleasing background. Pay attention to your remote presentation environment, and both your audience and storytelling will benefit.

Keep Your Camera at Eye Level

Next, check your camera level. Are you looking straight into the lens, as if you were seated across from a friend and sharing a relaxed one-on-one conversation? Or are you looking down into your camera as the laptop sits on a desk? Or up into the lens above a large monitor? Storytelling through a camera lens means making your remote and in-person communications as similar as possible.

If the camera is too low, you'll be looking down on your audience. Get some books under the computer to raise that camera up to eye level. If your camera is above your head, and you can't lower it, you'll be looking up at your audience, which feels very strange. Raise the chair or sit on a cushion or two in order to speak straight into that camera. Eye-to-eye connection is what makes both in-person and remote presentations comfortable and confident.

Bad Lighting Is Bad Storytelling

For many speakers, poor lighting is the biggest challenge to successful in-home presentation. Even the most valuable talk deteriorates when the audience can't see the speaker's face due to a dark room or overexposure from windows in the background. If we can't see you, we won't hear you, and your talk goes straight to our *low-value* or *no-value* bins, regardless of its content. Do not neglect proper lighting. You can easily brighten up your in-home studio at little or no cost, applying just a bit of effort and ingenuity.

Rule number one is no windows behind you, day or night. Cameras will always autobalance to the brightest spot in the frame, meaning they expose for sunlight in the background and plunge your face into darkness. At night, windows reflect your computer screen or room lighting and create an awkward distraction. If you have to record in a space with windows, turn to face them or draw the curtains.

Remember that outside light conditions change throughout the day. If you set up your in-home studio at 9:00 in the morning to record using natural daylight, but then you don't get to work until 3:00 in the afternoon, your light will look entirely different. If it's sunny one minute, it may be cloudy the next, completely altering your on-screen image. Try to avoid windows altogether. Close the blinds and control the room lighting yourself.

My favorite trick is to find two bedside table lamps, remove the shades, and place them on or behind your desk, at 45-degree angles, just out of camera range. These will light up both sides of your face softly and evenly, allowing your camera to properly balance and giving attendees a good look at your eyes and the passion they convey. If you have them available, add another floor lamp to light up your background, and another in front of you for an even wash across your recording space. This is a great no-cost strategy to recreate studio lighting in your home or office.

If possible, invest in a couple of basic LED panels and cheap tripods to mount them on. A variety of simple, affordable DIY kits are available through any number of tech retailers and will significantly alter the quality of your image for an online audience.

Overhead lighting is also unpleasant to a remote audience. Because they point down at the top of your head instead of forward toward your face, overhead cans or spotlights cast deep shadows under your eye sockets. Bald speakers get severe light bounce, and darker hair will reflect hot spots. Try to turn off any direct overheads. If one switch controls every bulb in the ceiling, unscrew those bulbs that are directly above you, and allow the others to fill your room with light.

Maximize Bandwidth

If you prerecord your talk using local capture, Wi-Fi bandwidth is irrelevant. But if you deliver your talk live on any web portal (Zoom, Webex, RingCentral, Microsoft Teams, Google Hangouts, GoToMeeting, Nextiva, etc.) then bandwidth can become your bitter enemy. Drop-offs in service will degrade your image and audio, and loss of signal could freeze your screen or cut you off in the middle of your talk. Any weak link in your home or office connection can disrupt your storytelling.

To minimize these risks, connect your computer to the modem or router using a hardline rather than relying on wireless service. A $10–$15 ethernet cable will always be more reliable and less susceptible to bandwidth degradation than Wi-Fi or Bluetooth. At the same time, even with a strong, consistent signal, most meeting applications automatically compress both your video and audio across the stream. A hardline connection can offset a bit of that compression, improving your image and audio for your audience. Once you finish your talk, you can just as easily return to Wi-Fi and keep that cable handy for your next presentation.

If you have to go wireless, maximize bandwidth by setting up your presentation space as close to your router as possible. Signal degrades quickly over distance; the farther away from the source, the lower your signal quality and capacity. Ten feet and 25 feet can net very different results.

If it's available in your area, consider upgrading your network speed. Most urban and semiurban service providers charge an extra $10–$30 per month to open a much larger up/down signal. For most speakers, this is a relatively small investment to ensure your talk looks and sounds its best. You can usually purchase this faster service on a month-by-month basis, turning it on and off as needed to remain cost efficient.

Finally, command full use of your home's data pipe by closing all other applications that connect to your system and eat up streaming strength. If your family is at home or demand is particularly high, slowing down your connection speed, ask everyone to disconnect from the network while you speak. Be certain no one is watching Netflix, YouTube, Amazon Prime, TikTok, Facebook Watch, etc., as video streaming services consume the most bandwidth. Maximize your signal to avoid hiccups.

Interact with Your Audience

The final strategy for better storytelling through a camera lens is to create more interaction with your viewing audience. Great remote presentation requires you to include your attendees in your talk. Involve the audience regularly, even more than you might in person. Invite them to participate instead of simply lecturing at them the entire time. Ask questions, encourage them to vote in live polls, play a game, and solicit real-time comments in the chat bar. Find creative ways to make your online listeners a vital, engaged part of your valuable content. The more you involve your attendees, the more they will feel as if they are sitting right in front of you.

Here are a few interactive ideas that are equally applicable and encouraged in both your online and in-person talks:

1. Ask Hand-Raiser Questions

Do you think there's no reason to ask a question if you won't be able to see or hear the audience response? Think again. You won't see their online reaction, but your question serves as a tool for inclusion, directly involving your viewers in key aspects of your core content. Asking questions in your remote presentation maintains the feedback loop, getting viewers engaged and demonstrating that they are as much a part of your talk as you are. Their participation makes them the stars of your story.

Open with a question, or ask for audience participation in the first 30 seconds. Remember, your audience wants to feel recognized, respected, and valued the moment you begin to speak. What better way to prove that value than by soliciting their opinions? Getting viewers to mentally raise their hands early (answer a poll, agree to a premise, etc.) establishes passion and connection.

2. Solicit Live Q&As

Virtual presentations are typically lengthy lectures, a droning one-way street, with a camera lens creating separation rather than connection. Every time you break out of your content to ask your attendees a question, you initiate a two-way conversation and reignite the online connection. You may not see the heads nod or the hands go up, but you and your audience will both benefit from the interaction.

Take advantage of modern applications like Slido, which allows viewers to submit questions or comments as you speak. Designate times during your talk to stop and review submissions, then answer a question or respond to a thought before moving on to the next part of your script. Opening additional communication channels to the audience makes your talk feel more connective and inclusive.

3. Use an Online Polling Tool

Polls work well in online presentations because they elevate the experience and input of the attendee, allowing them to influence your talk by sharing their valued opinions. Numerous polling tool applications are easily integrated with the most popular event platforms: Poll Everywhere, Vevox, Slide, DirectPoll, and dozens of others allow you to put a question on the screen, then ask viewers to respond via their smartphones or laptops. Everyone sees poll results in real time, creating a stronger connection between you and your audience.

4. Pause for a Check-In

Even the most intelligent and savvy attendee can easily be distracted by any number of competing stimuli or mentally drift away. How can you be certain your audience has heard, understood, and internalized the important point you just made? Take a moment to pause the content and check in with your online viewers. Checking in regularly with your guests helps ensure nothing vital gets missed, and allows a distracted viewer the opportunity to catch up or reaffirm what they just heard.

Remember my Chapter Fourteen advice on embracing the pause? When you finish explaining or demonstrating a valuable benefit, stop the flow of information. Encourage another hand raise to strengthen that recognition. Or ask your audience if they clearly understood the benefit in the data you just offered. "Did you all recognize what a difference that's going to make in your daily operations flow? How many of you think you can put that capability to work right away for your teams? If you're still not totally clear, or have a question, drop it into the chat window!" Guide any attendees still not entirely clear on your message to more information on how to fill in the blanks.

Checking in regularly with your audience helps remind you that there are living, breathing, value-driven humans out there listening to you speak. And it reminds your online attendees that you are delivering this talk for their glory and success.

5. Turn to #twitter

Twitter can boost audience engagement during your presentation, allowing you to interact with attendees as they respond to your ideas in real time. Create a unique hashtag for your talk, then ask viewers to send out tweets throughout the presentation using your hashtag. Collect those tweets with an application tool like Everwall, and you can gather and share how viewers are positively responding to your content. Tweets can work like a crowd of people; when onlookers see a group engaged in something, they are motivated to go check it out for themselves.

Of course, this takes confidence that your talk is strong and on point. If so, using #twitter as an interactive strategy in your presentation can extend reach and influence beyond the moment or people in that virtual room.

6. Tell a Joke or Two

Jokes are subjective. Some people tell a great joke, while most (myself included) are mediocre at best. Here's a secret: Jokes don't have to be particularly funny in order to succeed with an audience. As long as a joke is appropriate for *all* audiences, the right groaner can grab attention as successfully as something that elicits a genuine laugh. Even a deliberate dad joke can alert your audience that you plan to have fun with them instead of taking yourself and your content too seriously.

A 2017 *Journal of Social Psychology* study found that (appropriate) humor signals confidence and competence, which in turn increases the joke-teller's status.[54] Good or bad, humor can play a fundamental role in shaping interpersonal perceptions and hierarchies within groups, improving people's perception of you in a professional setting. Told with self-deprecation and humility, even a silly or weak joke can help your audience see you in a more human light. If you're willing to have a little

---

54   Bitterly, T. B., A. W. Brooks, and M. E. Schweitzer. "Risky Business: When Humor Increases and Decreases Status." *Journal of Personality and Social Psychology* 112, no. 3 (March 2017): 431–455. https://doi.org/10.1037/pspi0000079.

fun, even at your own expense, you have an opportunity to make your talk relaxed and casual rather than just another corporate pitch.

—— 7. Get Your Slides into the Audience's Hands ——

Recent advances in technical distribution have created applications like Beamium, which lets guests access slides on their smartphones. Instead of forcing your viewers to passively watch your deck click past, you can invite them to actively assess your visuals in high resolution on their own personal devices. This can be even more beneficial in live settings where screens are not always clear, text may be too small to read, or distance from monitors makes for challenging viewing.

—— 8. Use Props ——

Incorporating simple physical props in your remote presentation can be a great way to grab audience attention, re-engage your guests, or add impact to your content. Place a few objects on your desk, within easy reach. Each time you show a new item to the camera, you break that camera barrier and add a moment of connection with your viewers.

Props are fun. And they play directly to the golden rule of presentation, "Don't tell us, show us." There is a marked difference between *talking* about antenna placement on a mobile phone and *holding up* a mobile phone to point out why those antenna locations can be challenging. You can describe a glass as being half full or pull out a pitcher of water and fill your glass to overflowing.

I recently placed an array of precut fruit and vegetables in covered dishes on my desk along with a blender. During a Calm[55] meditation break in our session, focused on health and better food choices, I loaded my blender and zapped up a smoothie while yelling over the sound of the whirring blades. It was fun, silly, and a great way to add a moment of levity to an otherwise heavy session.

In Chapter Eleven, I described showing tiny sensors to guests at a trade show. But the CEO's story really came to life when he passed one of those sensors around the room. Attendees showed a visible increase in sensory connection to our story by engaging with that tiny sensor

---

55   https://www.calm.com/.

for themselves. That wouldn't be possible in a virtual session, but if you were to hold that sensor up for them in comparison to a normal, everyday object—like a pencil—your audience would appreciate that tangible prop interaction.

If you want to watch an expert combination of props and jokes, seek out videos of comedian and writer Demetri Martin. Martin is a master of visual humor who often uses a cheap easel and flip pad to show wildly unskilled drawings that make the story he's telling hilarious and land with brilliant visual impact.[56]

— 9. Get Your Audience to Repeat Key Information —

In a study on memory at the University of Montreal, researchers found that repeating information boosts a person's ability to retain and recall data.[57] Ask your audience to orally repeat something you just said, and that piece of information becomes stickier and more memorable. This may seem awkward at first, but there are effective ways of making your request feel normal and appropriate.

If I tell my viewers that an application can reduce mean time to resolution by 70%, I might follow that assertion up by saying, "Think about what that could mean in your daily operations. 70% reduction! Say it with me—'70% reduction. 70% reduction.' That feels really good, doesn't it?" I have repeated a key value takeaway and helped my attendees to internalize that value for themselves, whether or not they actually repeat what I just said.

For in-person presentations, consider offering a small reward or gift to the attendee who correctly repeats something important you just said. I've had great success tossing out small bags of M&Ms for correct responses: "I just told you how much we speed up mean time to resolution—what was that percentage? 70%—exactly! M&Ms coming at you." You say it first, then get them to say it back along with you.

56 Martin, Demetri. "Flow Charts." Facebook, October 15, 2019. https://www.facebook.com/watch/?v=345944479510736.

57 University of Montreal. "Repeating Aloud to Another Person Boosts Recall." ScienceDaily. October 6, 2015. https://www.sciencedaily.com/releases/2015/10/151006142422.htm.

───── 10. Extend Focus with Physical Interaction ─────

In 2015, the Consumer Insights team of Microsoft Canada (using a research source called Statistic Brain) showed that humans generally lose concentration after eight seconds, faster than goldfish do.[58] While this science is disputed, normal human attention spans are a very real barrier for any speaker delivering a talk. TED limits its presenters to a maximum of 18 minutes, and peer-reviewed journals suggest that there is a decline in students' attention 10–15 minutes into lectures.[59] If your talk lasts 30 minutes, you want to consider ways to break up your content and reset the audience's internal attention-span clocks. A great way to do that is finding opportunities to get your audience in motion. Many of us are kinesthetic learners, meaning that we incorporate new information more reliably through movement or hands-on experience. Even those who don't require kinetic engagement for learning can quickly reach maximum saturation while sitting still at their home or work office desk all day long, listening to session after session and reading countless slides off a computer screen.

Any change in your viewers' physical activity can re-engage and refocus their attention. Hand-raiser questions require physical activity. A good joke can create laughter, a physical response. I like to ask my audience to grab a pen and piece of paper and write something down, maybe a list of the last three things they ate or their top five desert island movies. That gets them active. Then I find a way to tie those written responses in with some aspect of my content.

Be creative and varied by leveraging several kinetic elements across your talk. Bang the table for emphasis. Yank out a hair to elicit a pain or smile reaction. Take a sip of whatever drink is in front of you. Get viewers to look up a URL on their phone. Ask your audience to stretch, scream, or take a moment of physical action that resets their internal attention-span clock.

---

58   McSpadden, Kevin. "You Now Have a Shorter Attention Span Than a Goldfish." *Time*, May 14, 2015. https://www.time.com/3858309/attention-spans-goldfish/.

59   Bradbury, Neil A. "Attention Span During Lectures: 8 Seconds, 10 Minutes, or More?" *Advances in Physiology Education* 40, no. 4 (December 2016): 509–513. https://doi.org/10.1152/advan.00109.2016.

OLIVIER BODART

Climate and Environment Artist | Author | Media Creator
"Risk Areas" (Zones á Risques), *Éditions Inculte*, Roman, 2021

When I initially planned to go to places where natural disasters had taken place and to recover the materials that would form the heart of my box sculptures (roots, volcanic ash, everyday objects), the goal was not to create novels or objects of art, but to discover the stories these fragments of reality were destined to tell. Stories of geography that had lived its own life, and of the human beings who experienced that life firsthand. My own story as an artist and writer drove me toward these wild and chaotic locales, as if I was taking part in an investigation: geological, compassionate, personal.

It seemed that the central question around which my literary and artistic activities revolved was not simply "What is the state of our planet?" but rather "What is the state of our narrative?" By revealing the stories that we tell ourselves, I discovered a desire for augmented reality through narration and began to produce works that perpetuate the stories of these places and people and the disasters they witnessed. This effort has brought me into reality, allowing me to be more present in the world, with more compassion and understanding.

Circumstances create storytelling. The elements and materials I collect from natural disaster sites are placed "under seal" within my box sculptures. Those sculptures are then connected in a single narration that forms my latest novel. Part fictional, part autobiographical, this new story incorporates factual events and travels to real locations, brought to life through fictional sculptures and photographs created by my main character. This process unfolded quite naturally for me as a writer and visual artist.

When process and story combine, the results can be rewarding, beautiful, even shocking. Find your story, and you find your reality.

CHAPTER SIXTEEN

ICEBREAKERS

"I HAVE NO IDEA HOW TO BEGIN MY TALK."

I hear this complaint so often. A speaker knows their topic, their title, and what they are expected to include, but they are stymied at how to take the first step. As we discussed in Chapter Eight, the opening of your talk should instantly involve and inspire your audience, grabbing them with commitment and value. And as we discussed in Chapter Nine, you have to demonstrate that value and investment straight out of the gate. That's a lot of pressure on a speaker, and it's the reason many don't know where to start.

When you step on stage, your first words open a doorway to the story you want to tell. Some doors work better than others, and every speaker must learn their best door through trial and error. We call these doors "icebreakers," and I want to share a few that can help ease you into your content and establish rapport with an audience the moment you hit the stage. Try a few of these icebreakers to see if one or two solve your "How do I begin my talk?" challenge.

Write an Introduction for Someone Else to Deliver

Ask another person to introduce you and talk you up a bit before you step into the spotlight. Rather than starting cold, a host's introduction gets the audience warmed up and receptive, giving you a runway to take over once the ice is broken and your credibility is pre-established.

As you write your introduction for someone else to deliver, don't overdo the job title, merits, statistics, or awards. Keep it personal and focused on your passion and experience instead of on your résumé. Include why you are excited to deliver the talk and the benefits and values you want to provide for everyone in the room. Here are two introductions for the same speaker; which do you find more appealing as an audience member?

> Diane is VP of operations for the Central US and leads the customer experience team. She has an MBA from Cornell and was featured in last year's *Forbes*'s "100 Female Executives to Watch." Diane's essays on client engagement and direct marketing have been published in *Business Today* and she is a frequent guest on CNBC. Please welcome Diane.

Or,

> As VP of operations for the Central US, Diane is a dedicated mentor and visionary for increased female leadership. She helps companies like ours to encourage inclusivity in establishing leadership and shows us how diversity can create amazing customer relations. You've probably read Diane's essays and seen her on TV; we're so lucky to have her with us today to help with new approaches to D&I, to make us stronger and more successful, and to answer questions about creating real power in our organizational structure. Please help me welcome Diane!

An audience is less interested in your CV than in who you are as a person. Your bona fides are already clearly established, initially by the bio in your session abstract, then again by the fact that you are the one delivering the talk. Your attendees don't need a third bio repeat in your introduction, and neither does the person introducing you.

Write an introduction about your audience and your value to them instead of about yourself. Whoever makes that introduction on your behalf will enjoy delivering it, and you'll minimize the pressure of proving your own merit the moment you step up to the microphone.

Open with a Quote

Taking the stage with a quote can be an effective icebreaker that gets your audience learning and feeling smarter before your content even gets underway. A meaningful quote can speak volumes, especially if there is a direct connection to you or your topic. Find a quote that relates to the spirit or value in your talk, and let it launch you into your presentation.

I advise against angry, upsetting, or negative quotes. But a wise proverb, funny observation, or insightful perspective will instantly capture your audience's interest. Imagine stepping on stage or joining the Zoom session with thought-provoking concepts like these:

> The most valuable lesson I ever learned came from Ralph Waldo Emerson: "Do not go where the path may lead; go instead where there is no path and leave a trail." We're all on a path toward energy independence. We're all blazing a trail to profitability in renewables. We're going to take Emerson's advice this afternoon.

> "The way to get started is to quit talking and begin doing." Does anyone know who gets credit for that quote? Walt Disney. And me, because in the next thirty minutes I'm going to tell you why it's time we stop talking about getting AI into our labs and start using AI in our patient diagnoses right now.

> Author Steve Goodier said, "It is a mistake to think that moving fast is the same as actually going somewhere." Today I'm going to talk to you about speeding up your data center migration to the cloud. And I'll show how that migration pays off only if you know why you're doing it and where you want data migration to take your organization.

Finding the right quote to suit your story may take some time and research, but it serves several masters by immediately engaging the viewer, supporting your thesis, and giving you a clear and simple way to kick off your talk.

Enter with a "Hand Raiser"

In the previous chapter, I encouraged querying your audience within the first 30 seconds of your presentation. Consider moving that up to become your icebreaker. Opening with an interactive ask can be powerful, and it sets the tone for the rest of your talk, especially if that ask contains a challenge or vision. Instead of worrying about how to set up your theory and prove credibility, the right question cuts directly to the chase:

> Raise your hand if you feel as productive and effective working from home as you ever did from your office.

> How many of you can tell me exactly why your brand is a key player in the race to 5G reality?

> Who here would add 50% to your budget tomorrow if you could triple your operations output in three months?

Keep your opening question positive and enticing rather than negative and off putting. "How many of you want to be more productive and beat your own quotas by 300%?" is positive and enticing. "Who has been frustrated by this pandemic and thinks their organization doesn't have enough to show for the past seven quarters?" is negative and off putting.

Ask questions you know most people will raise their hands in response to. The whole point of a hand raiser is to get majority audience engagement and unified group involvement. A good query first elicits a wide reaction, which then results in a type of positive peer pressure: "Hmmm, everyone else is raising their hands, I guess I should too," or "I didn't really think about the question, but now that I have, yeah, I do want that!" Ask colleagues to help you develop questions from multiple perspectives in order to find the one with the highest likelihood of encouraging everyone to get those hands in the air, physically or figuratively.

Start a Story ... but Don't Finish It

Books are delicious when one chapter ends by demanding you continue on to the next. How many nights have you planned on turning out the light at the end of the page, then you realized two hours have passed? Your talk can use the same tactic in its icebreaker. If the setup story is strong, your viewer will happily stick around for a satisfying conclusion.

Open with a compelling tale, but leave it incomplete or unresolved, with a promise to return later in your talk. If you do this well, your audience will be hooked and follow you through your journey to hear where it winds up. Here are a couple of split-story examples to help get those creative juices flowing:

> I heard about a woman who was killed by her pet parrot. He didn't peck her to death or anything so gruesome or Machiavellian. He accidentally poisoned his owner with gas while she was taking a nap. Amazing story, right? It gets even more amazing, I promise. And I'll tell you why a bit

> later. But this murderous parrot is a perfect metaphor for my
> session today. Because I want to share what happens when
> we get so internally-focused on our own way of doing things
> that we forget about our clients and their needs. We end up
> accidentally killing valued business relationships.

This is a delightfully macabre story from 1899 that opens a talk with a sense of fun and humor, ties to the speaker's topic, and ensures the audience will stick around for the fascinating conclusion. Since you won't get to hear that conclusion, it turns out the parrot was a "fume fiend," a "feathered victim of the gas habit."[60] In an effort to get his daily high, this avian would pop the tips off the owner's gas stove burners and inhale until he collapsed on the floor. The owner wasn't so resilient. After a few days without contact, relatives broke open the door and found their deceased daughter lying next to a stoned and half-dead mini murderer. The bird recovered, and while the coroner was still in the house, the little malcontent was caught trying to turn on the gas again. This is great storytelling!

Here's another story starter that encourages an audience to stick around for the juicy ending:

> A tiny startup called Kytch sued the billion-dollar manufacturer
> of McDonald's notoriously broken ice cream machines. Kytch
> sold a small device that hacks those machines so McDonald's
> owners can self-diagnose and fix their own equipment.
> A company called Taylor, the machine manufacturer for
> McDonald's, tried to copy the Kytch device and sabotage

---

60 "Feathered Gas Fiend: Parrot Killed His Mistress by Tearing Off a Burner." *Mariposa Gazette*, vol. XLV, no. 20, October 28, 1899. https://cdnc.ucr.edu/?a=d&d= MG18991028.2.31&e=-------en--20--1--txt-txIN--------1. (UCR California Digital Newspaper Collection).

> its business. It's a classic case of the dog chasing its own tail, then biting it off. And it has a sweet ending. But first, I want you to think about all the external technologies integrated with the security in your own data center. Are those devices making you more secure or sabotaging your business? We're going to look at the difference in this morning's session, taking a McDonald's-level view.

This little-known news story leads directly into the core topic, intriguing the listener as an opening icebreaker that promises a worthy conclusion later in the presentation. I'll share it with you now. An independent analyst showed that Taylor was deliberately keeping the McDonald's ice cream machines fragile in order to drive additional repair contracts. They're now under a restraining order—David may beat Goliath after all. Kytch cofounder Jeremy O'Sullivan equated Taylor (and McDonald's) with Lockheed Martin's challenges over the F-35 jet: "Does Lockheed want to finish this airplane? Or do they want another $100 million contract to fix some component on the old one?"[61]

Break Some News, Big or Small

A news release, anticipated product launch, or surprising reveal can be an effective icebreaker and easy doorway into your talk. Humans are curious and inclined toward FOMO. When something new or interesting happens, your audience wants to know they're in on it. News doesn't have to be international or earth shattering to be interesting, relevant, and compelling as a method of getting your audience engaged.

Again, keep any news story fun or inspirational rather than chilling or

---

61 Greenberg, Andy. "The McDonald's Ice Cream Machine Hacking Saga Has a New Twist." Wired. November 23, 2021. https://www.wired.com/story/mcdonalds-ice -cream-machine-hacking-kytch-taylor-internal-emails/.

heartbreaking. Your goal is to elevate attendees, not bring them down the moment you step on stage. Here is a news item from the day I'm writing this chapter and how it could connect with and lead into a talk I'm preparing to deliver next month:

> In the Uber this morning, I read that, after fifteen years of infighting, James Brown's estate was sold for $90 million. That money is going to fund Brown's longtime dream of scholarships for kids in his home state of South Carolina.[62] This great story made me think of our own twenty-five-year delays in achieving local, performance-based transportation here in our state. Like Brown's family, we've waited too long to do what needs to be done. Now I don't have a world-class music library to fund this effort—do you? We may not have $90 million, but we have raised $28 million, and we know what that money can do for our citizens right now. We just have to get to work and stop letting the perfect be the enemy of the good.

Sharing a news story as the opening to your talk is only successful if it directly relates to or connects with your topic and intent. Random red herring stories with no correlation to your presentation are to be avoided. Here's a recent opening statement that actually made me do a spit take:

> Did you hear that a woman in Brazil gave birth to octuplets this morning? Amazing, right? Hi, I'm James, and I'm here to show you the latest bumpers with recovery hooks, built-in winches, and a front skid plate for bashing the toughest trails.

---

62 Abraham, Mya. "James Brown's Estate Sold For $90 Million Following 15-Year Legal Battle." Vibe. December 28, 2021. https://www.vibe.com/music/music-news/james-brown-estate-sold-1234641800/#respond.

Oh, my dear James.

Opening your talk with news of a product launch can be equally effective, but only if that launch is truly game changing for your audience or the industry. What may feel exciting for you or your brand ("Welcome to Insights Version 8.6!") may be less exciting or important to your viewers ("I don't see much difference between Version 8.6 and 8.5—besides, I'm still back on 7.2.") If an announcement is your icebreaker, make sure it's worthy of that lead position:

> According to Gadgetec, aluminum-ion batteries with graphene structure are about to revolutionize the battery market. Three times the energy, 20%–60% faster charging, no overheating, and 2,000 recharge cycles with no degradation in performance. All based on a metal that's abundant, cheap, and easy to access. If you're as excited as I am for this breakthrough, let's get started.

Most speakers don't get the opportunity to make a major announcement in their talks because C-levels prefer to reveal those launches themselves, usually at dedicated press events. By the time you're cleared to share the news, it may no longer be news. But, if you are a C-level reading this book, ignore the last sentence, and go share that launch!

You may also consider sharing a news story from another company that directly correlates to or positively impacts your own brand. Here is an announcement I used to open a talk in summer 2021:

> Yesterday, Mark Zuckerberg announced Facebook's shift to the metaverse, what he calls "an embodied internet, where instead of just viewing content, you are in it."[63] According to

---

63   Newton, Casey. "Mark in the Metaverse: Facebook's CEO on why the social network is becoming 'a metaverse company'." The Verge. July 22, 2021. https://www.theverge.com/22588022/mark-zuckerberg-facebook-ceo-metaverse-interview.

> proponents, Meta will be the new platform we use to socialize,
> conduct business, and do anything else that can be done in
> virtual, 3D spaces. But what about privacy, lifestyles, behaviors,
> and the work we do each day? The wider our social connection
> surface spreads, the harder it is to control and the more we need
> embedded solutions like the ones I'm going to share with you
> this afternoon.

This launch story from Zuckerberg had a direct connection to my client and their latest developments and made for a perfect icebreaker and opening springboard into my scheduled speaker content.

Ask for a Simple Participation Exercise

In the last chapter, we looked at the benefits of kinetic learning. I urged you to alter your audience's status quo with simple physical-response activities to break up your content and reset the viewer's attention-span clock. If you get your audience to engage in such a physical activity the moment you step on stage, this can be an excellent ice-breaking strategy. For example:

> Before I start, turn to the person sitting next to you and offer
> them a high five. If you're social distancing these days, give them
> an air five instead.

Not everyone will participate, and you may notice an eye roll or two, but you're shaking up the room and creating a bit of buzz to dispel the awkward moment of walking out into the spotlight. Then creatively connect the activity to your topic:

> Why did I ask you to acknowledge and even physically connect with that human being sitting next to you? Because we're going to spend the next twenty minutes looking at partnership—the partnership your organization and mine have to engage in if we're going to successfully bring connected education to every student as part of the global network. We start small—by high-fiving our friends and colleagues—and the stakes go up from there.

Rather than struggling to find the right words to kick off your presentation, try a simple, physical ask that is quick and undemanding for the audience:

> All right, everyone, stand up if you've been to Disney World in Florida. Keep standing if you've also been to Disneyland in California. Stay up if you've also been to Disneyland Paris. Remain standing if you've visited Disneyland Tokyo or Hong Kong or Shanghai. If you're still standing, how do you even have time for a job with all this travel? Okay, everyone sit down. What we've just seen is that, societally, many of us choose to spend our hard-earned money on the same priorities. When we coalesce around one agreed-upon way to invest—like going to a theme park—we experience and achieve something shared and universal. Sharing experiences lets us do more in partnership than we can do separately. You've probably heard the "African proverb" that says, "If you want to go quickly, go alone. If you want to go far, go together." There's no proof that proverb came from Africa, but maybe it came from Disney.

That icebreaker managed to combine physical participation with a quote—two for one! Not all activities have to be deeply meaningful. Some speakers open with creativity just to break the ice and shake up a room full of tired conference attendees. I've seen speakers have great success by walking out on stage and immediately asking their audience a series of yes/no questions. Responses can be verbal, hand raisers, or stand-up, but participation is usually quick and comprehensive.

Even generic questions are great if they create a tiny connection back to the purpose of the presentation. Here's a creative idea I heard a colleague use with her audience:

> Did you ever watch *The Love Boat*? Can you name three stars of *The Love Boat*? Wow, you're as old as I am! How many of you don't even know what *The Love Boat* is? Great, now I feel even older. In this session, we're going to set our hearts for adventure and our minds on a true romance. And here's how …

I love that. Questions can also tie directly to session or meeting content. If you're at a conference, try opening with a series of questions based on information your audience has heard previously and that directly plays into your talk:

> In this morning's keynote, Liz talked about the single biggest impact on Kubernetes's success—do you remember what that impact was? Exactly! Then, Harold gave us the impressive growth in container adoption over the last four quarters—who can tell us what that percentage was? Right! Finally, Joanne sent us off with a quote from one of the most beloved innovators of all time—who was that innovator? Well done, everyone!

Introductions as Icebreakers

If you find yourself speaking to a smaller group, especially if it's to people who know one another, you can afford to be a bit less formal or have a little more fun with your audience. Standard practice in such small, intimate sessions can often be to ask everyone to introduce themselves before the content gets underway. Shake up that tradition by personalizing the exercise in ways that lighten the mood and entertain the room:

> Most of us know each other, but how well? We're going to find out. As usual, tell everyone your name, then tell us your favorite midnight snack, and the most useless thing you currently own. You're not allowed to say your spouse or your children. Let's start over here ...

Incorporating a little improvisation and group participation gets a familiar group of attendees thinking, smiling, and maybe groaning together. Feel out the room, and sense what your group is likely to accept and respond positively to. You might ask, "What item in a hardware store would you be?" or "What is your spirit animal?"

Don't worry about the potential loss of professionalism, and don't try to connect a topical corporate tie-in to this low-risk, simple opening engagement. The point is to break the ice by energizing the room and establishing a more casual talk, one that feels peer-to-peer rather than professor-to-classroom. One of my favorite introduction games is asking participants not to introduce themselves but to introduce the person sitting next to them using a manufactured bio, made up on the spot. This improv activity can elicit kindness:

> This is Rebecca. She works in HR and is super cool. She's brilliant, has a great smile, and makes the best snickerdoodles.

Or it can elicit a laugh:

> This is Bobby Bigdeal. He moonlights as a superhero, he can spit fire, and he's married to a beagle.

Creative openers like this only work in comfortable, supportive environments, but they are effective in taking the pressure off crafting the perfect first lines of your talk.

The next time you're thinking, "I have no idea how to begin," try opening with a connective or informative icebreaker that makes your attendees an active part of the conversation from word one. A good icebreaker can serve as an open door that your audience can easily step through on their way to your valuable core content.

LiSára Love
Entrepreneur | Songwriter | Founder of Sexy Sound Healing

As a kid, I often rejected the storytelling of others. My father was a movie buff, and I'd sit beside him in the theater feeling utterly exhausted after enduring an(other) emotional cinematic roller coaster in which I had no say. A precocious child, I was already writing poetry, lyrics, and my own stories ... perhaps I just needed to control the storyline. Perhaps we all do.

You and I are already natural storytellers. From childhood, we subconsciously create and internalize stories that color our perspectives, schemata, and ideas of what is and isn't possible in our lives. We play out these stories—good, bad, and ugly—every day in our personal and professional choices. Sometimes it's not better storytelling that we need; sometimes we need a better story to tell ourselves.

Enter sound healing. Sound brings stories to life; a scary movie is nothing without its accompanying soundtrack (insert your favorite bone-chilling screeches and werewolf howls here). Sound healing takes that a step further, utilizing specific frequencies that engage our physiology and induce various states of consciousness through brainwave patterns, where subconscious reprogramming becomes possible. Sound healing is a vehicle for us to consciously access the place where we can rewrite our old stories.

I guide C-level executives and private sound-healing participants toward deeper self-awareness, identifying and releasing the stories they've personally (or organizationally) been operating under. Together we evolve toward a new, personal place of innovation, where a better story awaits. It's like putting a preverbal storytelling pen back in the hands of a speaker and their audience.

Sound helps evoke the imagination and ingenuity that ignite better stories. The resulting intrinsic motivation arises from the sense of ownership we feel when writing our best possible narrative. Once we're free to tell our true story, we unlock our full potential. And our storytelling can then give others the keys to better their own stories.

CHAPTER SEVENTEEN

STORIES, QUOTES, AND ANECDOTES

WE'VE SEEN HOW CORPORATE STORYTELLING IS A POWERFUL, UNDE-niable blend of value, passion, and connection. We've learned strategies to turn a lecture into a conversation through stronger storytelling. Even if we experience glossophobia, we've learned steps to diminish or tame it as we speak. You don't have to love giving a public presentation, but you don't have to hate it either. An appreciation and respect for the opportunity to share your story, to bring benefit to a group of strangers or colleagues, is often enough to carry the day.

My first mentor as a professional corporate spokesman was a wonder-ful, kind, and ultra-talented man named Mark Brink who gave me the most valuable advice of my career: "Repeat after me—thanks for the mon-ey!" Mark was preparing me for those times when I didn't want to deliver a talk, wasn't in the mood to get on a plane, didn't care for my client, felt disrespected or undervalued, or wasn't feeling a connection to what I was saying or why I was saying it. Mark's point was that, simply by being asked, I was in fact being highly valued by the client. And that deserved my unerr-ing respect and appreciation in return.

Instead of complaining or neglecting my responsibility, it was my duty to find the positive in the occasion and to focus on the opportunity and audience instead of on my own insecurities and irritations. Sometimes just getting the job, keeping the job, and being paid to do the job is a good indicator that we are right where we're supposed to be. To this day, whenever I find myself whining about my work, I think of my friend Mark: "Repeat after me—thanks for the money!"

For years, colleagues told me, "Hey, you should write a book about all the things you've seen and learned at conferences and events!" I always said thank you, but I brushed it aside, knowing that this would be a book that perhaps tens of people might be interested in reading. Ours is an "insider" type of industry; the stories we find fascinating require specialized knowledge to have any impact. Sort of like free-form jazz.

A friend once told me, "Listening to free-form jazz is like watching someone else's home movies." That was how I thought of my personal stories from the professional speaker trenches—limited appeal to say the least. And definitely not the book I wanted to write.

Yet my trove of stories is deep and wide, gleaned through watching expert storytellers create messaging magic and the pain of watching unprepared and misguided speakers disappoint countless unfortunate audiences. I'd like to leave you with a few of the worthier lessons I've been lucky enough to learn. Hopefully, these instances of wisdom, weirdness, and wit will hold an additional lesson or two for you as well, getting you in your own storytelling mood.

There Are No New Ideas

In *Steal Like an Artist,* Austin Kleon says that every artist gets asked the question, "Where do you get your ideas?" The honest artist answers, "I steal them."[64] Because, in reality, every new idea is in fact just a mash-up or a remix of one or more previous ideas. As Paul Simon hinted at, the trick is not to be entirely original but to accept that your story can be engaging, inspiring, and valuable without reinventing the wheel. Your topic may not be new, but it will sound new to the audience because you are the one sharing it.

---

64   Kleon, Austin. *Steal Like an Artist: 10 Things Nobody Told You About Being Creative.* New York: Workman Publishing Company, 2012.

In Christopher Booker's (highly controversial) *The Seven Basic Plots: Why We Tell Stories*, the author posits that all ideas in storytelling ultimately fall under one of seven core themes that have existed throughout dramatic history.[65] Interestingly enough, all seven are easily correlated to corporate storytelling as much as to dramatic storytelling. In case you're unfamiliar with Booker, I'll share his original plot titles and character identifications, followed by sample adaptations of those plots and characters for our presentation strategy purposes:

1. Overcoming the Monster

Our industry (the protagonist) has been seeking the security technology breakthrough (which our organization has successfully developed) to defeat hacking conglomerates (an antagonistic force) threatening our companies and customers (the heroes and the protagonist's homeland).

2. Rags to Riches

We started in a tiny garage with no heat, a cheap sewing machine (poor protagonist), and a dream of creating the best athletic wear in the world. We moved from the garage to the penthouse (acquires power, wealth, and/or a mate), but the top brands tried to shut us down and almost succeeded (loses it all). Ultimately, we came out on top (gains it back, growing as a person as a result).

3. The Quest

The market was demanding energy independence, and we knew the only path was through easily accessible and renewable resources. We had to find and secure them (protagonist and companions set out to acquire an important object or get to a location) while fending off governmental resistance and protecting the communities where those resources exist. (They face temptations and other obstacles along the way.)

---

65   Booker, Christopher. *The Seven Basic Plots: Why We Tell Stories*. 2nd ed. London: Bloomsbury, 2019.

4. Voyage and Return

The cost and health risks of low poultry standards demand another solution. We went to the remote Andes (protagonist goes to a strange land) to work side by side with native farmers fighting a daily battle against famine and disease (overcoming the threats it poses) in order to perfect a new, humane, and completely clean system of serving mass demand for poultry. (Learning important lessons unique to that location, they return with experience.)

5. Comedy

People ask where a pizza-delivering, goofy-looking high school dropout like me got the idea for Skooble (light and humorous character with a cheerful ending), and I tell them, "Want to get inspired to make money really quickly? Try being a pizza-delivering, goofy-looking high school dropout!" (Triumph over adverse circumstances, resulting in a successful or happy conclusion.)

6. Tragedy

I became an addict when I was 28 (protagonist is a hero with a major character flaw or great mistake), which led to the loss of my company, valued at over $400 million. This plunged my 330 employees into unemployment (which is ultimately their undoing). I had it all, along with a solution that was going to change our sector forever. Now I try to help others realize their goals in a way I couldn't (protagonist evokes pity at their folly and the fall of a fundamentally good character).

7. Rebirth

I became an addict when I was 28, which led to the loss of my company and plunged my amazing 330 employees into unemployment. That was my wake-up call, the shock that turned my focus from making money to helping other addicts keep their companies, protect their employees, and bring their brilliant and necessary solutions to a hungry market. (An event forces the main character to change their ways and often become a better individual.)

How does your corporate story fit into one of these seven themes? Or maybe it doesn't. In 1895, Georges Polti wrote *The Thirty-Six Dramatic Situations* to identify the recurring plots we find in every story or performance.[66] Perhaps your story aligns less with Booker and more with Polti, featuring themes of deliverance, pursuit, revolt, rivalry, or ambition. Either way, it's likely your idea isn't entirely new, and that definitely doesn't matter. Even if your original idea was stolen—and they all are—it's the way *you* tell *your* story that counts.

Perceived Value Creates Real Value

Significant Objects was a literary and anthropological experiment devised by Rob Walker and Joshua Glenn, who demonstrated that the effect of narrative on any given object's subjective value can, in fact, be measured objectively. In 2009, Walker and Glenn purchased a variety of seemingly worthless and unrelated items at a garage sale for an average of $1.25 each. Some were even dented or damaged. Each item was then put up for sale on eBay, accompanied by heartfelt and well-crafted short stories by over 200 talented contributing writers. According to the research team, "We sold $128.74 worth of thrift-store junk for $3,612.51."[67] You can view these items and read their profit-driving stories on the Significant Objects website.

Their lesson is clear: Your product matters far less than the story accompanying it. Whatever you have to sell is less important than the corporate storytelling and passion you apply to selling it. To paraphrase my friend Bernard in his short essay following Chapter One, people don't buy the art, they buy the story.

Apple and Samsung continually duke it out for global smartphone

66 Polti, Georges. *The Thirty-Six Dramatic Situations*. Franklin, OH: James Knapp Reeve, 1921. https://www.books.google.com/books?id=PF5ZAAAAMAAJ&printsec=front cover&source=gbs_ge_summary_r&cad=0#v=onepage&q&f=false.

67 Walker, Rob, and Joshua Glenn. "Significant Objects … and How They Got That Way." Significant Objects. 2009. https://www.significantobjects.com/.

market share. In Q4 2021, Apple commanded 22% while Samsung measured 19%, for a combined total of 41% of all smartphones worldwide. The closest competitors were Xiaomi with 12%, Oppo with 9%, and vivo with 8%.[68] Now compare smartphone manufacturers by revenue, and the dominance story becomes astronomical. In 2021, Apple hauled in $196 billion, accounting for 44% of all global smartphone revenues. Samsung earned $72 billion, 16% of global sales revenues.[69] Does this extraordinary gap mean that Apple builds the best smartphones on the planet? Not necessarily.

Some expert tech reviewers argue that multiple Samsung and Google smartphone models are technically superior to Apple products. And, priced at $1,100, the iPhone 13 Pro Max was the most expensive model at retail. The explanation for Apple's ongoing dominance lies in the combination of a technologically celebrated product supported by strong corporate storytelling around perceived value.

Apple sells only premium devices, while many Android brands sell handsets at a range of price points, some of which are barely profitable or even lose money. Apple paints a dazzling picture of easy, dynamic interoperability between its devices, enabling a seemingly seamless shift on any app from mobile to home and from work to play. And that picture has only grown brighter and more enticing with the expansive "stickiness" of music, media, news, and data storage. Android devices are viewed as less interoperable and connective.

As Apple cofounder Steve Jobs said, "Innovation distinguishes between a leader and a follower."[70] In a saturated and highly competitive

68   Team Counterpoint. "Global Smartphone Market Share: By Quarter." Counterpoint Technology Market Research. February 8, 2022. https://www.counterpointresearch.com/global-smartphone-share/.

69   Chaudhary, Aman. "Global Smartphone Revenue Hits Record ~$450 Billion in 2021; Apple Captures Highest Ever Share in Q4 2021." Counterpoint Technology Market Research. February 25, 2022. https://www.counterpointresearch.com/global-smartphone-revenue-hits-record-450-billion-2021-apple-captures-highest-ever-share-q4-2021/.

70   Gallo, Carmine. *The Innovation Secrets of Steve Jobs: Insanely Different Principles for Breakthrough Success.* New York: McGraw Hill, 2010.

market, Apple innovation leads by capturing the market through perceived value as much as through technological strength. You can deploy this same storytelling methodology to your own talks. Capture your market by selling your story through perceived value even before the relative strength of your service or solution.

Ryan Williams and Three Anchor Stories You Need

I heard a great podcast conversation with Ryan Williams, media strategist and author of *The Influencer Economy*,[71] suggesting each of us should have three types of stories ready to tell at all times: the origin/tearjerker story, the authority story, and the pay my bills story.

The origin/tearjerker story describes an experience from your past where you had to overcome an obstacle in order to succeed and that now defines who you are today. This type of story resonates with everyone you ever speak to, connecting with them both emotionally and spiritually. Start by coming up with a couple of headlines from an experience that gave you a gift or taught you a valuable lesson. Here is one of my own origin/tearjerker stories I've used in presentations:

"Bullied to Beholden"

I was picked on nonstop in elementary school. Dave Mathers and Jack Nara were big bullies, twice my size, who faithfully promised to either "kick my butt" or "kill me" most every day from second through sixth grades. I found myriad creative ways to hide, escape, or make even bigger friends, like Dan Oliverio, a kind and gentle giant who shared my passion for Gilbert and Sullivan lyrics and who Dave and Jack didn't dare threaten.

---

71 Williams, Ryan. *The Influencer Economy: How to Launch Your Idea, Share It with the World, and Thrive in the Digital Age.* Oberlin, OH: Ryno Lab, 2016.

Thank you, Dan, for keeping me alive. Girls in my class picked on me because I was awkward, nerdy, and bad at sports. Fifteen years later, I married their ringleader. Thank you, Lorri, for eventually changing your mind. This daily harassment drove me to synchronize with my teachers, elders I respected and felt comfortable with who could protect me during recess and after school. Thank you, Mrs. Sullivan, wherever you are today. Out of necessity, I learned how to relate to and respect leadership, and by the time I passed the age of being bullied, I was adept at interacting with those more knowledgeable and powerful than me. And all of it thanks to Dave Mathers and Jack Nara. Thank you, Dave and Jack, for making me strong, and teaching me to survive and thrive.

Think through the life lessons you have learned, both good and bad. What experiences from your past might be associative and accessible to your audience today? Share something personal and from the heart, a story that instantly puts you and your listener on the same page. Something that says, "Hey, I'm just like you. We're in this together." The right origin/ tearjerker story will earn allies who are more receptive to your core content message.

The authority story displays expertise in your specific field. Describe how you helped make a project successful, or had a positive impact on a student, a coworker, or your boss. Share your time on a team that increased numbers and grew the organization. Remember, not all successes are extraordinary or exceptional; our most influential story is often a subtle victory. It may be small in scale but deeply personal, where heart is more important than fiscal profit. Here's an authority story of mine:

"Two Sessions with Frankie: Pain to Performance"

When Frankie walked into the speaker-ready room, she was
clearly in distress. I knew this coaching was going to be different
and more challenging than most. Frankie was a recent arrival
at the company, and she was working so many hours that she
could barely see her six-month-old daughter. Her husband was
a firefighter captain who spent weeks in the arid California
mountains on dangerous, smoke-choked ridges. Frankie was barely
keeping it together. She was also terrified of public speaking, but
tasked with an important breakout at an upcoming conference.
She needed my coaching support, but she needed a friend even
more. So instead of working, I ordered Starbucks delivery,
told Frankie to put away her laptop, and rescheduled my next
appointment. It was the first true "time out" Frankie had allowed
herself in weeks. There are times when helping someone get better
at what they do means helping them get better at where they are.
The next day, I opened another coaching appointment for Frankie,
and we spent ninety minutes on her content and delivery; she was
fantastic—not an expert speaker by any means, but relaxed and
confident. Getting the burdens off her mind and out in the open,
in a kind and friendly environment, had visibly lightened the load.
And she was able to speak without crying. Frankie's pain was still
very present, but through two very different coaching sessions, we
managed to make her pain subservient to her skills and expertise.

Authority stories don't always come from strength or power. Maybe
you feel as if you're not a great success in your career and that you've never
chalked up a big win or made what you would describe as a sizable difference. You still have an authority story worth sharing. Like my own elementary school teachers, you don't have to win a Fulbright to make an

extraordinary impact on a single at-risk student; you just have to protect and nurture a bullied kid.

A career isn't just pass or fail; the world needs both chiefs and soldiers, CEOs and middle managers. Don't sell yourself short because you were "only" a small cog in the wheel or a tiny slice of a bigger pie. Embrace your victories, regardless of their size. The best authority stories are little steps that eventually lead up big mountains.

The pay my bills story shares a problem you are currently solving for a customer and/or displays your most important business thesis. How are you personally and directly being useful to the economy or to the economy of others by making their lives better? Where you bring or add value is what earns you the credibility to lead the conversation. Here's one of my favorite pay my bills stories:

"A Region at Risk Proves Worthy of Independence"

I was hosting a series of events in Asia for a multinational corporation facing challenging times. The APAC-J team was underperforming, and corporate was threatening to shut their entire region down and consolidate under EMEAR control. The mood at these conferences was grim. Even worse, the regional VP leading these meetings was both furious and terrified, threatening his employees, badgering and belittling them in blame for what were clearly his own leadership shortcomings. Our events group got to work on two fronts: first, get the VP out of the room and on a plane back home to handle "more pressing demands," and second, shift the meetings from impossible delivery metrics to achievable performance victories. We quickly put together a series of committee breakouts that divided the full APAC-J team into small, focused groups, each built with a mix of expertise and a seasoned foreman at the helm. The goal was not to entirely overhaul the company's business methodology but just to reach the fiscal measurements EMEAR was demanding. Within a month, they were able to hit those targets. By allowing each specialized team to deliver on what it knew best, without the burden of groupthink or an abusive VP causing constant turmoil, the numbers climbed, and the region remained independent rather than being absorbed. Thousands of jobs were saved, and the VP was soon replaced by a more effective leader.

When you talk about why you do what you do, and how you earn money by serving and making money for others, you show an audience that you pursue your interests in a way that honors theirs. Create your three anchor stories, and you'll always have something compelling, personal, and passionate to share—in your talks and in any situation when a good story will serve the moment.

Risks Can Pay Off. Or Not.

Here are three of my favorite stories about taking big risks at an event.

In the late 1990s, speech-to-text technology was just beginning to burst onto the consumer market. I was hired to speak on behalf of a major tech brand hoping to get in on that burgeoning action. Unfortunately, my client's product was at least a year from reliable operation, but fearing loss of market share and competitive edge, they tossed up a desperate Hail Mary: me.

Over a series of powerful (and now long-gone) trade events like COMDEX and PC Expo, I would live demo a product that simply wasn't ready for prime time. Day after day, hour after hour, hundreds of attendees watched my speech-to-text software fail as often as it worked. Sometimes the tech performed perfectly; I'd dictate, "Hello.

I'm writing to you from the Las Vegas Convention Center, standing on stage in front of three hundred of my closest friends!" and a perfect text rendition would appear on the massive screen behind me. The audience would nod their heads enthusiastically and applaud this exciting new capability. Then I would take real-time suggestions to prove our demo wasn't canned. I might say, "Last night, for dinner, my friends ..." (I'd point at people and ask for their names) "Diane, Marty, and Narendra took me out for ..." (I'd ask others for food item suggestions) "pizza and sea bass." Up on the massive screen, our software would type out, "Last night for dinner, dying party and Nintendo shook me up for penis and sweet ass." My audience went from amazed and delighted to howling with laughter in front of me. There was no way anyone was going to buy this software.

But we sold thousands of units at $99 each—not because the software was perfect but because it was novel and worked "most" of the time. And because our audiences were having fun. The potential for future success felt legitimate, and my client was willing to risk looking foolish in order to inspire the customer. Our corporate story created an emotional response that made the moment memorable. To this day, over 20 years later, people still walk up to me at events to say, "Hey, aren't you that [BRAND] guy?!" You're damn right I am.

I once watched the global VP of marketing for a Fortune leader lose his job for taking a very costly and misguided risk to grab attention at a trade event. I was working for another exhibitor across the aisle, successfully connecting with flocks of visitors by telling a strong corporate story. The popular, historic brand opposite us was repelling guests by the hundreds and undermining their own credibility by hosting a costly and locally popular Berlin DJ (whom no one outside Berlin had ever heard of), pumping out meaningless jams with no storytelling connection to the company or its products.

Meanwhile, on a suspended catwalk above the DJ, a small crew of mediocre dancers flailed and gyrated without a hint of personality or enthusiasm. The confused audience was flanked by rows of empty demo stations and disinterested employees. Bored guests abandoned each performance in waves. This global brand wasted millions on a dreadfully expensive but unclear vision, built on glitz and flash instead of value or meaningful messaging. It was the wrong risk. Two weeks later, we read that this global VP of marketing had been terminated. Risk only pays off if it tells the right corporate story.

My final risk story netted both negative and, eventually, positive results for its company.

I watched an exhibiting organization get banned from a popular network security conference for illegally staging a mock political "rally" on the show floor. Without asking approval from event management or the authorities, the brand hired actors to "picket" their own booth, shouting slogans of protest for supposedly unsafe workplace practices and potential security threats. It was a bold move, designed to echo the conference theme and draw attention to security exposures all vendors and attendees were facing, but their "protest" theatrics were quickly shut down. The police were called in, and the exhibitor was booted from the event for two years. Bad risk, right?

Not so fast. The press picked up this strange story and ran with it, turning a negative and unintended result into more marketing exposure than the company could have hoped for or afforded. The brand realized far more visibility for their failed stunt than lost value from being ejected from the conference. Turns out they'd accidentally told the right corporate story after all, one that went beyond their products to become emotionally memorable through humor and controversy.

Agreement Is Overrated

Somewhere in our history, we decided, as a culture, that in order to truly trust one another, we should think the same way and agree on almost everything. In today's extreme political divide, we call that "living in the bubble." Humans are tribal by nature, preferring to circulate among those who believe as we do and to associate with people who view the world through the same tinted lens. Confirmation bias is more comfortable and convenient and less stressful than immersing ourselves in dissent and disagreement. But it is also a false narrative that doesn't ultimately serve our personal or communal needs. Agreement can be detrimental to corporate storytelling as well.

While a good corporate story should highlight alignment and mutual benefit, it should also spark a bit of controversy or a new way of thinking, challenging our audience to alter their status quo in ways they've never considered before. If your talk is afraid of challenging norms and ruffling a feather or two, it can easily fail by way of mediocrity.

A speaker aiming for absolute agreement underperforms for their attendees. Exercising extreme caution to avoid any chance someone in the audience might take umbrage is a weak and boring storytelling stance. This weakness is further exacerbated by fearful Legal departments that castrate presentations to avoid even the slightest risk of litigation or challenge. Words are forbidden and images are cut until every piece of the story is completely safe and deliberately whitewashed. When companies and their presenters are afraid to step out of line or rock the boat, audiences lose.

Giving a talk means standing up for something you believe in. Dissent can be a welcome aspect of that belief, particularly if you genuinely recognize how altering your attendees' point of view will serve them through important understanding and eventual benefit.

Trust your audience, and ask them to trust you. Challenge your viewer. Make them raise their eyebrow or question your tactics. Get them thinking and opening up to new approaches they might not have entertained before spending time with you. A great speaker never sacrifices value for agreement, because trust and passion usually lead to agreement by the end of a strong talk.

Emotion Triggers Recollection

Ask professionals to include emotion in their business dealings, and you might get a response like "Emotion has no home in business." Speakers resist including emotion in their talks, preferring to focus on corporate data and product details instead. After all, a presentation is about business, right? Not necessarily. When business and emotion happily coexist, the value of your communication will soar.

Emotion shows an audience your authenticity and a willingness to be vulnerable. Emotion makes us more human than corporate; the more our humanity is on display, the more alignment a viewer feels and the more likely they are to share our emotional response to the topic.

Emotion is also a form of sense memory. Jim Kwik, of Kwik Learning, says, "The brain processes a huge amount of data every day, so clearly it needs some kind of 'triage' system for determining what is important stuff that needs to be remembered, and what can be erased from our memory. One obviously good way of doing this is to prioritize information based on emotional intensity. Clearly, things we have a strong emotional reaction to are likely to be more important than ones we barely notice. Hence, if we are learning in a way that engages us, emotionally, then we are more likely to remember it."[72]

In her 2017 Futurism article "The Brain and Communication," Fabia Scali-Warner posits that every time our brain processes information, it can choose to follow a low road or a high road. "The low road is tied to the oldest part of the brain governing emotional responses, (bypassing) conscious reasoning and act(ing) as automatic responses to stimuli encountered before. The high road involves reasoning processes. Choosing this path requires more time for analysis, but favors strategic thinking and decisions focused on the long-term."[73]

---

72   Kwik Learning. "Did You Know? Emotional Intensity Prioritizes How Memories Are Stored." Facebook, July 10, 2019. https://www.facebook.com/KwikLearning/posts/information-combined-with-emotion-creates-memory-jim-kwik-the-brain-processes-a/10157665875109090/.

73   Scali-Warner, Fabia. "The Brain and Communication: Using Neuroscience to Control Our Messaging." Futurism. 2018. https://www.futurism.media/the-brain-and-communication.

Scali-Warner goes on to say, "Both the low and the high road are literally paths in our brain that are taken by the electricity carrying information through the nervous system. If the choice falls on the low road, the high road might process the information again. If the high road is taken as a first choice, there is no way to recall a low road reaction."[74] Simply put, as we speak, if we want a response from our listener's emotional brain, we need to grab their attention by conveying information emotionally rather than analytically.

Scali-Warner uses Facebook ads as an example of heuristic, low-road triggering. "For a Facebook ad to capture our attention and get us to click, it must stand out in a crowd of competing messages." Too much high-road marketing and we overanalyze; not enough and we scroll past. Low-road marketing triggers the emotion that then triggers the click. "When pushy salespeople want you to buy now and not a second later, they are trying to prevent your high road from kicking in and finding flaws in a seemingly excellent deal."[75]

Attach Your Message to the Moment

According to Dr. John Medina, author of *Brain Rules*, emotional intensity prioritizes how memories are stored. "Emotionally charged events are better remembered—for longer and with more accuracy—than neutral events."[76] One reason for this connection is the release of dopamine during emotionally charged moments, which Medina describes as a sort of "REMEMBER THIS!" sticky note for the brain, attaching a moment or statement to a specific memory.

Consider the doorway effect. I leave my office to make a cup of coffee, and by the time I reach the kitchen, I have utterly forgotten why I'm there. Scientists refer to this phenomenon as an event boundary, separating our memories into scenes that help us to organize personal experiences and

74   Scali-Warner. "The Brain and Communication."
75   Scali-Warner. "The Brain and Communication."
76   Medina, John J. *Brain Rules: 12 Principles for Surviving and Thriving at Work, Home, and School.* Seattle: Pear Press, 2014.

mental timelines in ways that attach a recollection to a specific time and place.[77] My office is one scene, and my kitchen is a different scene. As I cross from one room to the next, my mind stores one memory away and launches a new memory, connected to both where and when an event occurs.

As a speaker, you can take advantage of this natural memory-location phenomenon by tying your content to the specific time and place in which you're communicating with your audience. Look for ways to creatively associate the space you're speaking in to the topic you're speaking on, as in the following example:

> Here we are at the Mandalay Bay Convention Center in Oceanside E. Look up at those chandeliers. Now look down at that psychedelic carpeting. Feel that padded chair you're sitting on. Just like your home office, right? But next week you'll be back in that home office, thinking of what you just heard in our session. I want you to remember how you're feeling right now about transitioning toward meaningful ER restructuring. This psychedelic carpeting represents the powerful shift from random organizational strategy to streamlined, ordered pro planning for your medical team. These chandeliers are proof that money alone won't create differentiation or guarantee positive outcomes. And this cavernous room we're sitting in is a reminder that we perform better for our patients in calm, warm environments than we do in large, opulent spaces.

When you connect your message with your audience's current surroundings, you stimulate event-boundary association with your session content, helping to build emotional connection in your listeners' memory. Here's another approach:

---

77 Radvansky, Gabriel A., and Jeffrey M. Zacks. "Event Boundaries in Memory and Cognition." *Current Opinion in Behavioral Sciences* 17 (2017): 133–140. doi.org/10.1016/j. cobeha.2017.08.006.

When I flew into Denver this morning, I looked at the eastern face of the Rockies in a different way than I ever have before. These mountains are our reality today, a flat or low-rolling landscape that goes and goes and suddenly ends in an abrupt wall that shoots up in front of us. We're at the wall, here in Denver and across our entire sector. We can let that wall stop us, or we can leap over it by finally living up to our expectations and potential. What are you going to do, here in Denver and back with your teams? How are you going to make these mountains we're sitting in right now—physically and metaphorically—work for us instead of against us?

A more recent study suggests the so-called doorway effect is not as pronounced as previously thought and only occurs when the brain is working hard.[78] If you've done your job as a speaker, your audience's brains should in fact be working very hard throughout your talk and well after you've thanked them and left the stage. A smart presenter will use all available tools to assure their content remains unforgettable and stays in the viewer's memory as long as possible.

As an interesting sidebar, if you worry that your forgetfulness is related to age, allow me to dispel that notion. Equating faltering memory with advancing years is usually a false correlation. In most cases, aging does not have a direct effect on memory; instead, our loss of memory is simply because we need to use it less as we mature. The older we get, the more frames of reference we possess based on past experiences and the less we have to rely on gathering new context in order to process a moment or a piece of information. Now, don't you feel better?

78   McFadyen, Jessica, Christopher Nolan, Ellen Pinocy, David Buteri, and Oliver Baumann. "Doorways Do Not Always Cause Forgetting: A Multimodal Investigation." *BMC Psychology* 9, no. 41 (2021). https://doi.org/10.1186/s40359-021-00536-3.

ONE LAST STORY

Through more than 20,000 public talks at over 800 events, I've enjoyed a unique peek inside the heads of speakers and audiences of every type, age, size, ethnicity, perspective, socioeconomic status, persuasion, location, and expertise. I've learned what works in a presentation and what falls flat, what makes one talk successful and another forgettable. It's been a fascinating career that's given me inspiring insight into the world of corporate storytelling, and I'm equally excited and inspired to see what the next 20,000 opportunities teach me.

Corporate storytelling has been around, in one form or another, since the dawn of recorded time, and likely for millennia before that. When one hunter touted his skills or weaponry to another, or an elder sought to trade with a member of the neighboring tribe, I'm certain corporate storytelling skills played a big role. By the time John Deere delivered the first known use of content marketing in *The Furrow*, this practice of intimate value connection over hard sell had been honed and shaped for modern times. Since then, corporate storytelling has continued evolving over the last 125 years into our preferred mainstream communication practice.

You are the next great corporate storyteller. By leveraging even a few of the tools that you've gained from this book, your abilities to deliver value to an audience, to share your passion along with your pitch, and to create connection with your fellow human will combine to make every talk you give better and more successful from this moment forward. Keep adding skills, and your results will soar.

Glossophobia may never entirely vanish, but that's fine. Many of us live with stress, anxiety, phobias, and insecurities that we deal with daily through coping mechanisms and sheer bravery, refusing to let self-doubt undermine our lives. Public speaking works in exactly the same way. Add more corporate storytelling arrows into your quiver, and you'll subdue glossophobia every time.

Pay attention to other speakers. Learn from them and from the presentations you attend. Watch what others do right or wrong, and gratefully use both examples. Solicit the eyes and ears of friends and colleagues willing to help you create and deliver the best possible content for your viewers. Speak for the benefit of others instead of for yourself. And never hesitate to include your unique insights and personal experiences in every talk you give.

Because no matter your topic, your venue, your job title, or your audience, one truth will apply to every talk you ever give: nothing gets sold until the story gets told.

ACKNOWLEDGMENTS

A book like this doesn't come to life without the support, help, guidance, and expertise of so many amazing humans whose stories inspire and motivate me each and every day. At the top of the list (and every list) is Karen Multer, my best friend, foundation, heart, reason, and source of all things brilliant. Thank you for being my trusted proofreader and honest sounding board on this and every path to creation.

Equal thanks to our incredible girls, Julia and Avery, who sacrificed their father for countless hours of writing in the tiny office off the kitchen. You are our pride and joy in every way, remarkable storytellers in your own rights, and you remain the most beautiful stories we have ever told. This book could never have been written without my three loves.

To my fellow storytellers in these pages—Bernard, Brian, Cristián, Dave, David G., David K., Donald, Eileen, Heidi, LiSára, Michelle, Olivier, Paul, Sean, Stephanie, and Steve—thank you for your friendship, your generosity, and your wisdom, and for brightening the world with your exceptional talents.

My thanks to Sarah Busby, Graham Southorn, Bethany Davis, and Holly Akins for your proofreading prowess and wise direction. And gratitude to Julie Broad and her amazing team at Book Launchers for your invaluable expertise in helping shepherd this manuscript out into the big, wide world.

To my mom, Fran Multer, thank you forever and always for a lifetime of care, kindness, support, generosity, and limitless friendship. Thank you to Grandmother and Aunt Stephanie for setting me on a path all those years ago, though none of us knew it at the time. Gratitude to my mentors, compatriots, and fellow frequent fliers for days of onstage inspiration and nights sharing community and storytelling ideas around countless plates of food and glasses of wine. In particular, I want to thank the late, great Mark Brink for being my first corporate storytelling teacher, and Elaine Cohen, Joe Lauck, and Mark Norby for helping to light my path toward a passion-filled career I'd never recognized or considered.

My thanks to remarkable friends who offered valuable feedback and suggestions along this writing journey: Gary Taylor, Robin Bell, Larry Wyatt, Doug Weidner, Sonia Kupfer, Lindley Traynor, Paul Langford, Jennifer Andersen Langford, Andy Saks, Bryan Pray, Robert Strong, Don Colliver, Michael Thorson, Suzanne Smith, and Kent Smith.

A special thank you to the agencies that have allowed me to represent their valued clients: Arland Communications, Comedy Industries, Freeman, George P. Johnson, GetSynchronicity, Hay Moon Media, Live Marketing, MC2, Mindshare Advisors, MSM, Spark Presentations, Unipro, The Group, TPG, and Wilson Dow Group.

Last but truly first, my boundless thanks to the 100+ global brands and industry-leading corporate organizations that have trusted me with their stages and their customers. It's been an honor and a privilege to speak on your behalf, to coach your teams, and to write your corporate stories.

STORYTELLER URLS

Learn more about the talented, expert storytellers who have generously contributed their experiences and insights to this book:

Dave Arland   p 115   https://www.arlandcom.com

Olivier Bodart   p 176   https://www.olivierbodart.com

Bernard Derroitte   p 12   https://armstrongfineart.com

Cristián Gálvez   p 149   https://www.galvez.de

David Girolmo   p 162   https://www.broadwayworld.com/people/
                              David-Girolmo

Donald Goor   p 94   https://www.ccarpress.org/content.asp?tid=392

Sean Grennan   p 84   http://seangrennan.net

Brian Hilligoss   p 20   https://www.brianhilligoss.com

Michelle Juehring   p 49   https://www.kwqc.com/2021/10/28/bix-7-race-
                              director-recognized-emerging-industry-leader

Heidi Kettenring   p 127   https://www.broadwayworld.com/people/
                              Heidi-Kettenring

David Kovak   p 76   https://www.davidkovac.com

LiSára Love p 188 https://www.sexysoundhealing.com

Stephanie Rogers p 30 https://www.hipchick.com

Steve Schildwachter p 63 https://www.linkedin.com/in/steveschildwachter

Eileen Sweeney p 108 https://www.humankindpartnership.com

Paul Traynor p 41 http://www.haymoonproductions.com

AVERAGE SPEAKERS SHARE THE PRODUCT.
SMART SPEAKERS SHARE THE PASSION.

RISE ABOVE THE AVERAGE.

 Book Steve Multer to speak at your upcoming event, or to coach your speakers or teams: **stevemulter.com/contact** or **steve@stevemulter.com**

 Order discounted bulk purchases of this book for your company, employee speakers, guest speakers, or VIPs: **corporatestorytelling.com/bulk**

 Access corporate storytelling best practices and insider insights through Steve's videos and blogs: **corportatestorytelling.com/media**

 Join Steve's mailing list for exclusive opportunities, training giveaways, and the *Tuesday Tips & Tricks* Newsletter: **corporatestorytelling.com/contact**

CONNECT WITH STEVE ON SOCIAL MEDIA TO FOLLOW THE LATEST NEWS FROM THE WORLD OF GLOBAL EVENTS.

 /stevemulter

 @stevemulter

THANK YOU
FOR READING!

If you enjoyed **Nothing Gets Sold Until the Story Gets Told**, please leave a review on Amazon or wherever you purchased this book.

74408127R00138